Facilitating Conversations about Race in the Classroom

Learn how to facilitate conversations about race in the classroom, and why these discussions are such an important part of our work toward equity and justice. In this helpful book, Danielle Stewart, Martha Caldwell, and Dietra Hawkins cover everything from what you need to know to get started, to facilitation methods and techniques, to how to sustain your work. Drawing on their experience at iChange Collaborative, a group that works with schools across the country, the authors offer a plethora of compelling strategies and examples to help you hone your facilitation skills.

Specific topics include the importance of exploring your own identity, how to prepare yourselves and your classrooms for sensitive conversations, how to create class guidelines that create trust and allow vulnerability, and how to deliver explicit instruction in compassionate listening, sharing stories, and giving supportive feedback. The book also discusses the role of affinity groups in strengthening racial identities, building supportive relationships, and enhancing professional practices for educators of color and for race conscious white educators.

With the authors' practical advice, educators of all levels of experience and comfort levels will be able to address racial equity in schools or classrooms, so you can do your part to repair harm, educate, and ultimately transform society.

Danielle A. Stewart, EdD, is the president of iChange Collaborative. She is an innovative leader, organizer, educator, facilitator, and curriculum design expert in transformative racial equity education. She also established The Community Empowerment Foundation and In School Spirit to ignite positive school academic outcomes for students of color and pursue continued research in improving their experiences in school.

Martha Caldwell, MA, has 30 years of experience in education. She teaches, consults with schools, conducts seminars for teachers, and writes about education. Her interactive teaching method incorporates inquiry-based learning, social-emotional learning, identity formation (race, class, and gender), and ethics to achieve results that enhance empathy, stimulate critical thinking, and catalyze leadership development. She is a co-founder and director of iChange Collaborative.

Dietra Hawkins, PsyD, is a licensed clinical psychologist. Since 2006, Dietra had worked internationally with K-12 schools, government organizations, and behavioral health agencies. She is an author and frequent speaker for workshops addressing appreciative approaches toward system change, recovery-oriented systems of care, asset-based community development and inclusion, and the healing of racism.

Also Available from Routledge
Eye On Education
(www.routledge.com/K-12)

Let's Get Real, 2e
Exploring Race, Class, and Gender Identities in the Classroom
Martha Caldwell and Oman Frame

Identity Affirming Classrooms
Spaces that Center Humanity
Erica Buchanan-Rivera

Black Appetite. White Food.
Issues of Race, Voice, and Justice Within and Beyond the
Classroom
Jamila Lyiscott

Restorative Justice Tribunal:
And Ways to Derail Jim Crow Discipline in Schools
Zachary Robbins

Abolitionist Leadership in Schools:
Undoing Systemic Injustice Through Communally Conscious
Education
Robert S. Harvey

10 Perspectives on Equity in Education
Edited by Jimmy Casas, Onica Mayers, and Jeffrey Zoul

The Brave Educator:
Honest Conversations About Navigating Race
in the Classroom
Krystle Cobran

Facilitating Conversations about Race in the Classroom

Danielle Stewart, Martha Caldwell
and Dietra Hawkins

Routledge
Taylor & Francis Group

NEW YORK AND LONDON

Cover image credit: authors

First published 2022
by Routledge
605 Third Avenue, New York, NY 10158

and by Routledge
2 Park Square, Milton Park, Abingdon, Oxon, OX14 4RN

Routledge is an imprint of the Taylor & Francis Group, an informa business

Library of Congress Cataloging-in-Publication Data
A catalog record for this title has been requested

ISBN: 978-1-032-04298-5 (hbk)
ISBN: 978-1-032-02245-1 (pbk)
ISBN: 978-1-003-19135-3 (ebk)

DOI: 10.4324/9781003191353

Typeset in Palatino
by codeMantra

This book is dedicated to those who continue to believe that change is not only possible but closer than we think.

Contents

Introduction

Sabrina, a Black eighth-grader, tells her class that while she was perusing the jewelry aisle in a department store, she noticed the sales clerk was following her. "She was watching my every move, but she wasn't paying any attention to my white friends," says Sabrina. "I'm pretty sure she was watching me because I'm Black, and she thought I was going to steal something."

Miguel, a Latino student shares a similar experience about shopping with his friends. Margot, a white student, is surprised and dismayed. She had no idea how often Sabrina and Miguel felt the sting of negative racial stereotypes.

As the other students listen, Sabrina feels heard and believed. She's gratified that her classmates understand her experience and care about her feelings.

Experiences like Sabrina's are why we are writing this book. These are common occurrences, but these stories are not widely appreciated or valued. We are writing this book to help you create opportunities for students to share their truths and understand ways they can be part of systemic change.

Over the past decade, we have co-facilitated hundreds of conversations about race with thousands of school leaders,

DOI: 10.4324/9781003191353-1

teachers, students, parents, business professionals, nonprofits leaders, and community stakeholders. These conversations build the foundation for racial healing and transformational change through the lens of equitable relationships. We have found that unfortunately, most educators are not talking to students about race. All too often, conversations about race go awry, move underground, and are avoided completely.

By not talking about race, educators are missing an enormous learning opportunity. The deficit narrative about race in education must be undone and replaced with a new narrative about the strength and beauty of racial equity.

Breaking the Silence around Race

Dr Beverly Daniel Tatum is moderating a panel about diversity and inclusion education for early educators. She asks participants to silently reflect on their first memory of race. She asks them how old they were at the time. Most people were between the ages of three and six; some white participants were as old as 11. She asks them to reflect on how they felt at the time, and suffice it to say, the feelings ranged from nothing much to innocent curiosity, confusion, hurt, fear, anger, and sadness. Then she asks people to raise their hand if they talked to a trusted adult at the time. Only a few hands go up.

"That hasn't changed in the last fifty years," Dr Tatum says. "We still don't talk to children about race."

Bronson and Merryman (2009) describe a study in which white parents were asked to have explicit conversations with their children about race. Several families immediately dropped out of the study, and of the ones who stayed, only a handful followed through with the conversations. Instead, they reverted to comments like "Everybody's equal," or "We're all the same." These parents feared that drawing attention to skin color differences would actually make their children racist. They wanted their children to be colorblind. They believed it was best.

The study revealed that their kids weren't colorblind at all. Fourteen percent of the children said that their parents didn't like Black people, and 38% said they didn't know if their parents liked Black people or not. In the silence surrounding the topic, white children are often left to draw their own conclusions. Even when young children notice color and bring attention to it, they're often silenced.

In Martha's eighth-grade class, she asked students to interview their parents about how they taught them about race. The class discussion revealed that Black and Brown students talked about race with their families all the time. Their parents have to prepare them to face racism. Parents of color have to take measures to counteract the impact of negative stereotypes on their children. White students, on the other hand, reported that they rarely talk about race in their homes. Their parents echoed the ideas of the white parents in the study – the concern that drawing attention to racial differences would make their children racist.

There is no question that we need to talk about race and racism with young people, and young people need to be able to talk about race with each other. We need to normalize these conversations in our homes with our families, in our schools, with our colleagues, in our places of worship, in our state houses, and everywhere in our communities.

These conversations about race and racism strengthen racial identities for both Black, Indigenous, students of color, and white students who love fairness and justice. Black and Brown voices become empowered. They become resilient and able to resist the impact of racism and unearth the hidden notions of internalized racial indignities. White students also strengthen their racial identities in ways that cultivate their sense of integrity. They learn to listen to the voices of people of color and are empowered as advocates, allies, and co-liberators. They work through the emotionality of racial awakening and cultivate the strategic mindsets necessary to address and eliminate the structures and systems of racism.

Because we understand the support teachers need to start and sustain such conversations, this book offers a method they can use to build confidence and expertise. Our empathy-based communication model, known as Transformational Inquiry, developed over 20 years of practice, unifies rather than divides and yields transformation rather than confrontation. It builds identity-rich communities through learning experiences that integrate self-reflection, social interaction, intellectual frameworks, and dynamic action.

The Transformational Inquiry model deepens existing connections and builds new relationships. Educators know that relationships are the foundation for growth and change, in general, so this model is an extension of what we already know about relationships, social emotional learning, and transformational change. This pre-existing knowledge can be applied to foster racial healing and transformation.

Who This Book Is For

This is a book for educators who are seeking ways to engage students more deeply in learning and thinking about who they are, the world they live in, and the roles they can play in making a better world.

bell hooks (2015) says conversation is the revolutionary way of learning. Grace Lee Boggs (2012) says conversation IS activism. We know from facilitating hundreds of conversations about race with thousands of people that conversations are transformative. We offer a _model_ for facilitating conversations about race that educators can incorporate into their practice. We provide a _template_ they can use that allows students to start with themselves, to learn about their own families and culture and heritage, to focus on strengths they bring into our classrooms, and to share stories and resources to build shared knowledge. Through talking about race, our students become a community of knowledge builders and change makers. Our nation's history of racial suffering must be and can be reckoned with. As we face our history, we must face ourselves and each other. And this process begins and ends with conversations.

Transformational Inquiry and Identity Development

We start by consciously building an identity safe (and identity brave) learning community in which people courageously share the truth of their inner experience. Our method is called Transformational Inquiry and it addresses four domains of learning: personal, social, cognitive, and action. It begins in the _personal domain_ with self-reflection and self-exploration. It advances to the _social domain_ as participants share their stories, thoughts, and ideas with each other. Supportive feedback makes the sharing safe, and when sharing one's inner experience is safe, learning comes to life. In the _cognitive domain_, teachers act as facilitators and curators of information. They provide terms, concepts, and frameworks for intellectual understanding. Because of the work they've done in the personal and social domains, students are inspired to learn more. Finally, in the _action domain_, students take personal, collaborative, and/or political action designed to impact the world they live in.

Healthy identity development is not just an inside job. For a healthy identity to emerge, young people need to have their identities recognized, validated, affirmed, and supported. They need opportunities to explore who they are and who they want to become. They need opportunities to bring their personal stories and lived experiences of their racial identities to school and learn from and with each other.

In a Transformational Inquiry classroom, teachers and peers alike mirror their students' finest qualities and human aspirations. Students want nothing more than to be accepted in a community, so they eagerly acquire a social emotional skill set that allows them to connect and learn with their peers. Such a classroom creates a space for their budding identities to emerge.

The emergence of a healthy identity results in a cascade of positive outcomes, and these outcomes span the personal, social, cognitive, and academic domains. Students learn valuable communication skills: respectful listening, authentic sharing, how to give supportive feedback, and the value of empathy. As they mirror each other's experiences, they form deeper connections with each other. Attention to processing feelings allows their innate capacity for critical reasoning to emerge. As their identities become stronger, they develop the voice to speak out on their own behalf and on behalf of others. As they come to understand their capacity to effect change in the world, they find meaning and purpose in their lives. Along the way, they are motivated to acquire academic skills. They want to learn because learning generated from shared experience has meaning and purpose. Perhaps most importantly, they learn to love learning.

We have discovered in our work that when individuals have a safe space in which to share the ways their racial experience has shaped how the world perceives them and how they perceive the world, rather than causing divisions and controversy, the results are profoundly unifying. Conversations about race are the first step in changing the racial power dynamics in the classroom and beyond. By centering Black, Indigenous, and students of color's voices and creating environments in which they can bring their full selves into a learning community, stronger identities, more productive learning, and safer schools are the results.

Young people have always been the engine of change. In 2021 as we write this, young activists are bringing new urgency to conversations about race and racism. The entire nation is talking about race, and it's time for the conversation to move into our classrooms and schools. If we are to make progress, to end the disparities wrought by our nation's foundation in the history of slavery and genocide, we have to talk about the elephant in the room. Some say it's not an elephant; it's the room itself. Now is the time for every educator to embrace this journey, to develop and share your gifts. We have serious work ahead. It's not going to be quick or easy, but it can be done.

We begin by taking a deep breath, reflecting and acknowledging that our friends, colleagues, and students of color are hurting. We face the task of rectifying a long history of hurt and pain, a history of neglect, and a systems foundation designed to create compliance and lead Black and Brown bodies into the prison-industrial system. In a global pandemic that disproportionately impacts their families and communities, we are again forced to bear witness to cruel and senseless acts of violence against Black bodies. As we mourn the deaths of George Floyd, Breonna Taylor, Ahmaud Arbery, Trayvon Martin, Sandra Bland, Eric Garner, Tamir Rice, and so many others, our collective grief calls us to face 400 years of state violence that still visits inequity, fear, and intergenerational trauma on Black and Brown individuals and their communities.

Now is the time to heal together. In this book, we offer a pedagogical method and a set of communication skills you can use to help your colleagues and students talk about race in ways that will prepare them to be active participants in the creation of a more equitable future.

Layout of the Book

The book begins with how you can get started and then moves through facilitation methods and techniques. The final chapters are about how to sustain your work in racial equity education, recognizing that the work is rigorous and ongoing.

Chapter 1: What You Need to Know to Get Started. This chapter explores why talking about race in our classrooms is imperative. It outlines our guiding principles. It defines the difference between diversity, equity, and inclusion and explains why we focus on strengths and teach through the lens of resistance rather than oppression. It emphasizes why educators need to start with themselves and explore their own racial identity before attempting to engage in this work with students. Finally, we address the need to work in community with other educators dedicated to race equity in education.

Chapter 2: Understanding Identity. This chapter describes the differences between personal, social, and universal identities. We explore the impact of racial identity on students of color, emphasizing that educators have the power to counteract negative stereotypes and shift the narrative around race in education. We discuss three stages of identity development to describe how students move from a naïve stage of racial identity into the exploration stage, examining how exploration impacts students

of color as well as white students. Finally, we discuss the implications of student leadership in identity formation and learning.
Chapter 3: Cultivating Language to Talk about Race. Chapter 3 defines terms and conceptual frameworks that help students (and teachers) develop a more nuanced understanding of race, racism, and racial identity. We address the importance of taking an intersectional approach that brings multiple aspects of a student's identity into the room and not only their racial aspect. We define "levels of racism" that explain some of the ways racism operates in people's lives.

Chapter 4: Learning from Students' Stories. Chapter 4 explores typical patterns of experience based on the stories we have heard from students over the years. We outline patterns that both students of color and white students may have experienced or may be experiencing in these conversations.

Chapter 5: Creating an Identity Safe and Brave Learning Community. This chapter explores the relationship between social emotional learning and race equity education. It emphasizes how educators can build relationships with students and among students to facilitate learning gains. We cover creating class guidelines that cultivate trust and allow vulnerability. We discuss how explicit instruction in compassionate listening, sharing stories, and giving supportive feedback can strengthen relationships among students. We offer generative listening as an additional way to foster strong identities and counteract stereotypes. These fundamental communication skills lay the groundwork for learning gains in any area of education.

Chapter 6: Managing Emotional Processes. This chapter emphasizes the need to welcome emotions into conversations about race as racial experiences are frequently raw and emotional. We talk about how to move the process deeper, give supportive feedback, help students reframe negative experiences they may share, re-direct conflict, and manage patterns of participation. We discuss recognizing resistance as teachable moments and keeping students of color at the center of the conversation.

Chapter 7: Setting the Stage for Transformation. This chapter discusses how facilitators can prepare themselves and their classrooms for sensitive conversations. From the opening moment to the closing circle, we offer techniques we use to make these conversations meaningful and productive.

Chapter 8: Building Your Support Network. This chapter addresses the importance of intentionally cultivating a support network for any educator involved in racial equity work. We describe the role of affinity groups in strengthening racial identities, building supportive relationships, and enhancing professional practices for educators of color and race conscious white educators. We discuss the importance of building cross-racial relationships as a process for both healing the wounds of racism and cultivating leadership.

Chapter 9: Preparing to Launch and Lead. This chapter emphasizes that leadership development is central to the Transformational Inquiry process. We define leadership not as a position in a hierarchy, but rather a condition of knowing yourself and knowing your purpose. We call on racial equity educators to lean in and lead in their own spheres of influence wherever they may be. Research in identity formation demonstrates that leadership potential emerges with strong social identities. Ultimately, when we facilitate conversations about race, we are cultivating leadership. We emphasize, too, that leadership is central to the role of a race equity educator.

Chapter 10: Epilogue. This chapter re-emphasizes the urgent need to talk about race with students and faculties in schools to prevent harm, address harm, educate, and transform society. We review key strategies for developing facilitation skills for race equity education. It concludes with a call for more educators to find purpose in the work of racial justice, equity, and healing.

You Are Ready to Begin

We believe everyone is capable of facilitating conversations that matter. Since the beginning of time, humans have created forums – circles, council, and other sacred spaces – to share collective wisdom and visions of a better tomorrow.

We invite you to join our community of educators committed to racial equity and justice. We want you to know you are not alone. You are part of a movement. By plugging into a community, you will find the support needed to lead equitable conversations. You will find a place to share with others and get support for doing your own work. You will find colleagues to help you clarify your purpose and articulate why this work is imperative. You will learn to share your own story and build strategies to help your students tell their stories.

With practice and intention, you will become more comfortable with conflict, and learn to see challenges as opportunities. We are all learning and discovering together.

Welcome. Let's get started.

References

Boggs, G. L. (2012). *The next American revolution: Sustainable activism for the twenty-first century.* Berkeley: University of California Press.

Bronson, P., & Merryman (2009, Sep 4). Even babies discriminate: A NurtureShock excerpt. Newsweek. Retrieved from https://www.newsweek.com/even-babies-discriminate-nurtureshock-excerpt-79233

hooks, b. (2015). Moving from pain to power: Choosing the space of radical openness. Scholar-in-Residence Program, Eugene Lang College of Liberal Arts, The New School, New York. Retrieved from www.youtube.com/watch? v=cpKuLl- GC0M

1

What You Need to Know to Get Started

The evening Derek Chauvin was convicted of George Floyd's murder, we met with a group of teachers. Gloria, a Black kindergarten teacher, recounted a conversation she had with her 10-year-old son, Jared. "I'm worried about how the world will respond to the conviction," Jared said.

"How would you like for the world to respond?" she asked him.

"We don't want to make him an example, but we need justice for what's been done." He took a deep breath and continued, "But I worry about how he will feel locked up behind those walls."

Liz, a white high school teacher was moved by Gloria's story. "I'm amazed that your son can respond with empathy for someone who brutally killed a Black man," Liz said. "I'm also realizing that I've never had a conversation like that with my daughters." Liz paused and continued, "I guess I've never had to. I don't have to worry about how police violence could affect my white daughters like it could affect your Black son. Honestly, I've never been more aware of my privilege than I am right now."

"It means a lot to me to hear you say that," responded Gloria. "Thank you for being so transparent."

DOI: 10.4324/9781003191353-2

"I don't have the answers," Liz said. "I don't know what to say. I don't know where to start. I'm not sure what to say to my own children, not to mention to my students."

"My kindergarten students know what police officers are supposed to do," replied Gloria. "We have expectations for police officers, and young people are capable of understanding that this man did not do his job the way a police officer is supposed to. Not saying anything could be read as complicity. White kids need to be having these conversations too."

The demographics in our schools are rapidly changing, and the need to address and correct racial inequities is more urgent than ever. Students of color already make up the majority of students in our public schools, and by 2050, the population of the United States will be majority Black, Indigenous, and people of color. Yet our teaching force is 80% white (Characteristics of public and private elementary and secondary school teachers in the United States, 2020). We face a pressing need for educators, especially white educators, to develop the knowledge and skills necessary to guide our students through this imminent social transition. To successfully transition into a racially equitable society, we will need to talk about race. Educators need to know how to facilitate these sensitive conversations toward positive and productive outcomes so that students can achieve their full potential as individuals and as citizens.

Race is only one aspect of identity, but it's one of the first things we notice about someone. Some educators don't want to talk about race because they have been taught that bringing attention to racial differences only increases divisions. But research shows that avoiding the topic is what actually makes things worse because not talking about race influences racist mindsets. Well-intentioned avoidance of racism perpetuates racism, and we miss important opportunities for learning and healing. On the other hand, exploring one's racial identity and investigating race as a systemic force correlate to higher self-esteem, increased self-confidence, academic achievement, and ethical leadership in students of all races.

We understand race as a social construct, an illusion. The word race was once used to distinguish between nationalities: Italian, French, Spanish, and English were once considered different races. Biological notions of racial difference were invented to justify imperialism: the slave trade, Native American genocide, and limit Asian immigration. White supremacy was further institutionalized through Jim Crow laws, unfair housing practices, inequities in the justice system, and lack of access to health care, education, and citizenship, and denial of voting rights. These policies created the wealth gap, a persistent reality that continues to plague our society.

Race may be an illusion, but it's a persistent one, and one that has profound psychological and material effects on people of color. The consequences of race are as real as gravity.

We need to talk about race. Well-intentioned avoidance and silence about race denies the consequences of race, perpetuates racism, and undermines the many strengths and achievements made by the communities of color. To remain ignorant is to deny glaring social realities: the history, politics, and economics of racism. Even worse, when educators remain silent or purposely redirect the focus off of race, they deny the realities of the students standing right in front of them who are living and breathing the politics of race every day. Educators need to acknowledge the prevalence of racism in the lives of their students and recognize that it is perpetuated through society's institutional structures.

When we recognize inequalities in education, in the legal system, in housing, and health care, we can investigate these disparities so they can be corrected. We can highlight and embrace cultural differences with respect and admiration. Racial history emerges as a source of pride when seen through the lens of resistance and survival against difficult odds. We can't ignore that structural inequalities are affecting the personal biographies of our students. We can grapple with the complexities of socially constructed racialized differences, and so can our students.

Why We Need to Talk about Race

Catherine, a white teacher with 20 years of classroom experience, gave her fifth graders a survey to find out what they were most interested in learning. She discovered that her predominantly white students were intensely interested in issues of justice and fairness in the world around them. They wanted to learn about race and how they could contribute to creating a more equitable society. Yet Catherine felt unprepared to lead them in conversations about race, so she hesitated to follow up. "I feel inadequate," she said. "I just don't know where to start."

Teachers like Liz and Catherine feel ill-equipped to discuss race with their students. What if the conversation goes awry and devolves into confrontation? Avoiding conflict feels safer, yet in avoiding the issue, we miss out on real educational opportunities. The key lies in leading these discussions with the same thoughtfulness that guides other curriculum choices.

Racial identity is a lived experience for everyone, and it takes an emotional toll on the lives of all our students. For Black, Indigenous, and people of color, racism is experienced as an oppressive force. Researchers report that as much as 75% of bullying is bias related (Richardson et al., 2012), and when bullying is related to core components of a student's identity such as their race, the effects are even worse. Having a forum to talk openly about encounters with racism and experience adult and peer support can mitigate its effects.

We know supportive relationships with teachers help students learn, but so do relationships with peers. Healthy relationships in the classroom keep students engaged, and the benefits transfer into academic achievement. Yet students need to master a set of prerequisite social and emotional communication skills to keep their exchanges respectful and forge compassionate relationships. Clear ground rules for respect are needed, and these guidelines can and should be taught.

When students feel safe enough to tell their stories in a classroom, they can be accepted and affirmed by their teacher and their peers. When they hear each other's stories, they feel empathy and understanding. Telling their stories nurtures authentic relationships among them. When they share their personal experiences with prejudice and/or privilege, their differences are transcended through empathetic understanding.

Learning to talk respectfully about race and racism improves school cultures. After participating in a day of dialogue about how their race, class, and gender identities influenced their relationships, eighth graders in a Nashville public school took action to bridge the divisions among them. The eighth graders began intervening on behalf of other students, and their actions created a dynamic that resulted in a positive change in the entire school environment. After a similar unit at an Atlanta KIPP School, seventh graders initiated an anti-bullying support group.

To rise to the challenges of our times, students need to develop the skills to build relationships across differences. Through sharing their own stories and hearing the stories of people whose experiences may be very different from theirs, their voices are empowered; they gain appreciation for diverse cultures and life experiences; and they learn perspective-taking and critical thinking skills. These skills transfer into greater academic performance.

How to Talk about Race

Empathy is the North Star of the Transformational Inquiry Method. Empathy, or the ability to "feel with" another person, to imagine what it feels like to be in that person's shoes, and take their perspective, is a key ingredient of human relationships, but also foundational to critical thinking. Understanding how deeply our experiences are impacted by our racial identities is the first and most urgent step in building our capacity to address racism. We live in a system that advantages some racial identities and disadvantages others, and we form racialized notions of ourselves, whether conscious or unconscious, through childhood conditioning, family backgrounds, the neighborhoods we grew up in, experiences in school, religious indoctrination, media coverage, national and international politics, and other ways of socialization. Unpacking our own conditioning, bias, and past experiences with race helps us be more available to help our students explore their experiences.

Too often, as educators, we feel we have to know the answers before we ask a question. But in conversations about race, we often don't know the answers. What we really need to know is how to ask the right questions. We need to know how to elicit students' stories, protect their vulnerability when they are courageous enough to share them, and teach the social skills they need to navigate these conversations. We need to understand the common patterns our students encounter and how to extrapolate their stories to create a curriculum that addresses the broader phenomena of racism and resistance in society. We need to incorporate reflections of their perspectives in what and how we teach history, literature, math, science, and the arts.

What Educators Need to Know

Before embarking on the work of facilitation, acquiring some foundational knowledge is necessary. Besides knowing how to facilitate sensitive conversations, educators need to know why these conversations are important, a fundamental history of race and resistance, and some race-based patterns of experience they may encounter in their students as they move into this work. It helps to develop a clear pedagogy in case you are called upon to defend the rationale of your curriculum. There is a rich tradition of critical pedagogy (Duncan-Andrade & Morrell, 2008; Friere, 1970; hooks, 1994; Wink, 2011) and extensive research in identity formation theory to support this method (Côté & Levine, 2002, 2016; Erikson, 1968; Tatum, 1992, 2017). Positioning your work within educational theory and practice strengthens your confidence.

Set Your Compass: Guiding Principles

Every educator needs to define a set of guiding principles. Our work is informed and guided by four underlying concepts. These principles lay the foundation for every conversation we facilitate and provide a positive, appreciative focus on strength-based learning.

Every human being is a genius. We believe each student has a gift to contribute to their learning community. Each of them brings rich family traditions and cultural histories. Our work as educators is to recognize each student's unique and individual personhood in light of the understanding that their individuality is impacted by the racial identities they bring to school. Understanding how their lives are impacted by race is central to their development as ethical human beings. Our goal is to bring out their innate gifts, affirm their intelligence, validate their experience, and strengthen their identities. Our job is to help them cultivate their gifts and realize their potential. Their racial identities are intimately tied to unique, individual identities, because being who you are and being true to yourself is the most intelligent thing you can do. But social identities can get in the way of that intelligence expressing itself. When racism is internalized, it limits potential.

We believe equity and inclusion are the ground of intelligence and reason. The stronger and more confident you are about who you are, what you know, and what you believe, the more intelligent you become. Stronger identities are associated with self-determination and agency, higher academic performance, and success in life.

Learning is an emotional, social, and cultural process. Learning is not only an intellectual activity. Learning is always emotional. It's exhilarating to learn; it's exciting and fun. Teachers live for those light bulb moments and frequently describe them as the most rewarding part of their work. They can see that moment in their students' faces when everything falls into place. Nothing compares to the thrill of learning.

Yet sometimes learning is a struggle. Learning can also be frustrating, difficult, and fraught with conflict. It can feel overwhelming when things don't make sense, when other people understand something, and you just don't get it. Either way, learning involves a transformation that is always emotional, so welcoming our students' felt experience into our classrooms is fundamental to this work.

Learning is also social. It's never done in isolation, but rather in community with others. Even when you're alone reading a book, you're still interacting with another human being, the author, and all that author brings to the text.

Learning is a cultural transmission, so we begin by acknowledging that our students learn through the cultural identities they bring to school. These identities can be "read" as another kind of text, another kind of literacy. As educators, we have the power to create learning experiences that affirm, validate, and strengthen our students' cultural identities and experiences.

Learning is also cultural in the sense that it is value laden. Schooling as we know it has both an explicit and a hidden curriculum. The ideology that manifested racism is still embedded in the structures of schooling today, and we see it manifested in the so-called achievement gap, the discipline gap, the numbers of Black and Brown students absent in advanced placement classes, graduation rates, and college admissions.

Social emotional learning combined with identity-inclusion practices lead to ethical development and cultivate leadership potential. Social emotional learning theories and methods are abundant in the literature, but there's something missing from just about every approach to social emotional learning. SEL skills cannot be learned in a vacuum. They need a context and teaching such skills in the context or race and relationships can provide the missing link. That's where social emotional learning finds practical application.

Conversation is the revolutionary way of learning. We learn from listening to and sharing ourselves with others. Conversational learning recognizes race-based power dynamics and levels the playing field by making patterns of discourse more equitable. Equitable conversations empower student voices and build trusting relationships. The work of racial equity can only begin when we know how to talk about race with respect, honor, and hope.

Ethical leadership emerges from strong identities. Erikson wrote that integrity is the end point of identity development. Kohlberg (1976) believed that only a small minority of people reach the stage of identity in which ethical reasoning emerges. Research in identity formation demonstrates that leadership emerges from strong personal and social identities.

In our work, we don't define leadership as a position in a hierarchy. Leadership emerges from identity strength, and you don't have to be a school administrator to lead. You can lead from right where you are. We define leadership as being who you are and having the confidence to act on that knowledge. Ethical leaders are strategically focused on the power they hold within their sphere of influence. These leaders have a sense of purpose grounded in a commitment to something larger than themselves. Students and teachers alike find purpose and meaning in their commitment to equity and justice.

These principles keep our work focused on passion and purpose. We know before we start what we believe about every person we encounter.

Racial Diversity, Equity, and Inclusion Defined

We hear a lot about the value of diversity, equity, and inclusion education, but what do those words mean? Understanding the difference between diversity, equity, and inclusion helps us navigate these critical conversations in ways that build on students' strengths and create positive outcomes.

Diversity is a fact. The term diversity refers to the demographics of a group and is measured by the different racial identities of the people present in the room. In conversations about race, diversity matters. The first step in preparing for conversations about race is to assess the demographics of the group. For a rich exchange of information, the more diversity, the better. Ideally, we want a critical mass of voices that represent the lived experiences of each identity. If there are only one or two Black or Brown students in a class, we want to be sensitive to their position. These conversations can be awkward for them. It's not their job to educate their peers. Their experience can be raw and emotional, and our first priority is to protect them from harm.

Some teachers combine their classes to achieve a critical mass of voices, so these students don't feel put on the spot. "I appreciate teachers who let me speak when I want to, but they don't expect me to be the spokesperson for my race," says Grace, an Asian American student. Sophie agrees, "I sometimes feel this pressure to be the Black spokesperson. Anytime the subject of race comes up, everyone looks at me."

When a class is predominantly white with only a small minority of students of color, the focus of conversations about race may be better focused on exploring the impact of white identity, dominant culture norms, and white racial conditioning.

Attention to diversity involves assessing the needs of the group. What is the range of identities in the group? Who is here? Who is not here? What are the strengths each student brings to the group? What are their challenges? What do they already know? What do they need to learn? What is their comfort level? What do they need as individuals, and what do they need as a learning community? What curricular resources will support their development?

Inclusion is an act. Inclusion is a set of intentional behaviors that can be as simple as making eye contact, greeting a person in the hallway, or asking them about their day. Inclusion is expressed through genuine concern and authentic curiosity about a person's lived experience based on their race. It involves a willingness to listen and learn from them. It may include invitations to lunch, to collaborate, or to lead. Inclusion is the secret sauce behind the increases we see in innovation, productivity, and engagement among diverse groups. Inclusivity results in a feeling of belonging and creates group synergy. When people feel their contributions are valued, they want to give more.

Attention to inclusion involves creating a safe and brave learning community. What do students need to feel safe? What guidelines can we create to make each student feel a sense of belonging? How can we recognize their unique gifts and contributions? How can we validate their experiences? How can we affirm their cultural heritage? How can we support their individual and social identity development?

Equity is an investment. Achieving racial equity requires an investment of time, attention, and resources. It can mean using one's privilege to spread awareness or interrupt racism. It can mean risking one's comfort to make a difference. For educators, it means investing in students' academic success and personal well-being. It means getting to know them both inside and outside of the classroom. Kevin, a Black student, appreciated the investment his white history teacher made in him. He knew she cared about him and consequently, he worked hard in her class.

Attention to equity also involves an investment of time to learn. It means acquiring new skills and knowledge. How have my students' lives been impacted by race? What stereotypes have they encountered? How do their racial identities impact their learning? How does my curriculum support their racial identity development? What do I need to learn to be a better race educator? What is the impact of my racial identity on my relationships with them? How does my own social location inform the way I teach and my expectations of my students?

Making an investment in racial equity is a long-term commitment.

Teach Resistance and Resilience, Not Oppression

There's far more to the story of Black and Brown Americans than oppression, so balance the narratives you teach about racial oppression with the rich history of excellence and accomplishment. The lives of people of color are centered around resilience, love, energy, joy, and survival. Their experience has not occurred in a vacuum of despair. They have overcome near insurmountable obstacles and have still found ways to be joyous, grateful, and gracious.

When you teach about race, maintain an appreciative lens. Stay focused on strengths, resistance, and resilience. Trust that we can unpack and unlearn racism, and by working together, we can empower the next generation to change the trajectory of history.

Start with Yourself

Before you can teach others about racism, you have to do your own internal work. Cultivating mindfulness about your own racial identity is a fundamental skill in developing cultural agility. In *The Courage to Teach*, Parker Palmer (2017) says we teach who we are. The first step is self-inquiry – exploring your own identity experiences. As you do, you develop metacognitive awareness, which allows you to witness your own thinking. This helps you become aware of your own unconscious biases and uproot prior social conditioning around race. Unconscious bias is simply a part of life and becoming aware of it is an ongoing process. At first, recognizing your biases may feel uncomfortable, but once you get the hang of it and move past self-judgment, catching your unexamined thoughts as they emerge from your unconscious mind will be rewarding.

If you are an educator of color, it's likely that you've already done a good bit of racial identity work. Your life experience has required you to grapple with the impact of racism in your life and learning. Educators of color frequently enter the teaching field with the purpose of making the educational experiences of students of color easier than theirs were. They understand the work of identity formation and the energy it takes to overcome racial oppression through firsthand experience. They will find support in learning to use their stories to create opportunities for their students to explore their own personal narratives.

White educators, on the other hand, may just be beginning the work of racial identity exploration. The work of unearthing unconscious bias, understanding racial privilege, and the impact of dominant conditioning is where they need to start. This can be difficult work, and as such, we encourage you to build your capacity for feeling discomfort. One aspect of racial privilege is that it allows white people to remain comfortable, and this resistance to discomfort is what makes conversations about race difficult. To facilitate conversations about race, recognizing your own discomfort as a form of resistance to learning is necessary so that you can recognize it in your students and help them process through it.

To build a capacity for discomfort, you have to be present for your own feelings. This is true for all educators. Schooling is based in white middle-class culture, and as such, it conditions us to think instead of feel. We have all learned to devalue our emotions and elevate our intellects. Allowing feelings of discomfort to surface and being mindful of these feelings is the only way to process them. Feelings buried alive never die. They live under the surface of our consciousness and sabotage our thinking. The distorted thinking that emerges can only cause harm. To think rationally, we have to live in awareness of our feelings.

Racism itself is irrational. It cannot be reasoned away. It operates through the repression of the very human emotions that connect us to each other. Only through sitting with feelings of grief and sadness, guilt and shame, anger and powerlessness, can we process our way through the pain to power. Allow your feelings. Honor them as the sacred signals they are, telling you that all is not well. Hold space for yourself and for those you love to process and transmute these difficult feelings so they can inform and enlighten you.

Find a Community of Resistance

To fully engage in racial equity work, you need to find your people. We strongly recommend that you surround yourself with a community of like-minded people who share your commitment to racial healing. Start or join a racial equity book club, an educator of color affinity group, or a race conscious white educators' group. These groups operate as sanctuaries for educators to share stories, experiences, ideas, and resources. Such communities are invaluable ways to encourage and support each other's development as racial equity educators and reinforce the race conscious work we are called to do together.

The nature of oppressive conditioning is that it alienates us from others, but it also alienates us from ourselves. And by its very nature, teaching can be an isolating profession. All too often we go into the separate worlds of our classrooms, cut off from the support and nurturance of other adults. As a result, teachers are often hungry for connections with each other. Sharing stories and building relationships with other teachers is highly invigorating and important for sustaining us in our work. Teachers find renewed inspiration and appreciation for their craft through close connections with each other. Teachers routinely tell us that the most rewarding aspect of racial equity work is the close connections they make with their colleagues. For years, teachers we work with have maintained close connections through our affinity groups for educators of color and our race conscious affinity group for white educators (Educator Resource Groups, 2021). In these groups, they continue to share resources and support each other.

We stress the need to consciously and deliberately develop a network of supportive relationships with like-minded educators. Affinity and ally relationships overcome the isolation inherent in the present structure of the teaching profession and to counteract the oppressive structures of social identities like race. Racial insensitivity, whether conscious or unconscious, intentional or unintentional, is common even in the most progressive of environments. We still live in a world struggling to overcome our personal and collective histories. We need to know we are not alone.

Building a network of supportive, equitable relationships is imperative in challenging oppression. We need deep connections with other educators to sustain our work. We need relationship networks with people who share our racial identity experience and can support our empowerment. We also need networks of allies across differences with whom we can communicate fluidly to achieve our common purpose. We need each other to build our capacity and strengthen our commitment, but we also need to work together to build a movement. Affinity groups are good places to practice facilitated conversations that allow for vulnerability and build trust.

References

Characteristics of public and private elementary and secondary school teachers in the United States: Results from the 2017–18 National Teacher and Principal Survey. (2020 Apr). National Center for Education Statistics. Retrieved from https://nces.ed.gov/pubs2020/2020142.pdf

Côté, J. E. & Levine, C. G. (2002). *Identity formation, agency, and culture: A social psychological synthesis.* London: Lawrence Erlbaum Associates.

Côté, J. E. & Levine, C. G. (2016). *Identity formation, youth, and development: A simplified approach.* New York: Psychology Press.

Duncan-Andrade, J. M. & Morrell, E. (2008). *The art of critical pedagogies: Possibilities for moving from theory to practice in urban schools.* New York: Peter Lang.

Educator Resource Groups (2021). iChange Collaborative. Retrieved from https://www.ichangecollaborative.com/services/educator-resource-groups/

Erikson, E. H. (1968). *Identity: Youth and crisis.* New York: Norton.

Friere, Paulo (1970). *Pedagogy of the oppressed.* New York: The Seabury Press.

hooks, B. (1994). *Teaching to transgress: Education as the practice of freedom.* New York: Routledge.

Kohlberg, L. (1976). Moral stages and moralization. In T. Lickona (Ed.), *Moral development and behavior* (pp. 31–53). New York: Holt, Reinhart & Winston.

Palmer, P. (2017). *The courage to teach: Exploring the inner landscape of a teacher's life.* Hoboken, NJ: Wiley & Sons.

Richardson, S. T., Sinclair, K. O., Poteat, V. P. & Koenig, B. W. (2012). Adolescent health and harassment based on discriminatory bias. *American Journal of Public Health, 102*(3), 493–495.

Tatum, B. D. (1992). Talking about race, learning about racism: The application of racial identity development theory in the classroom. *Harvard Educational Review, 62*(1), 1–24.

Tatum, B. D. (2017). *Why are all the Black kids sitting together in the cafeteria?* New York: Basic Books.

Wink, J. (2011). *Critical pedagogy: Notes from the real world.* Boston, MA: Pearson Education, Inc.

2

Understanding Identity

A group of eighth graders sit in a circle, pens and paper in hand, ready for writing class to begin. "Close your eyes and think of a challenge you faced in childhood," Martha begins. "It can be something you've overcome, or it might be something you're still trying to figure out. It doesn't have to be the worst challenge you've ever faced, but it can be if that's a story you're willing to share."

After a few minutes of reflection, the students write a paragraph describing their challenge. Then in small groups, they share their stories.

Marion shares that he moved from a mostly Black school to a school in which he was one of the only Black students when he was in fourth grade. He had never been around white people before and felt like he didn't fit in. Candace tells about getting her hair cut when she was in the sixth grade, and the "popular girls" laughed at her and called her a lesbian. Miguel started school speaking Spanish and struggled to do schoolwork in English. Michael's attention issues made it hard for him to keep up in math and he felt stupid. Kimberlie said she wasn't accepted by the white kids at school, and the Black kids in her neighborhood accused her of "acting white." Lila's best friend in elementary school stopped sitting with her at lunch because she wanted to sit with the Black kids.

DOI: 10.4324/9781003191353-3

Almost every story the students share is about the pain of social exclusion. Almost every story is about the deep human need to belong.

When we facilitate workshops with students or adults, we frequently explore their "challenge stories." This activity gives participants an opportunity to share their stories in a safe and accepting environment and practice compassionate listening. By sharing their childhood challenges, they form deeper connections, learn to better understand each other, and begin to build relationships.

Among educators, we frequently hear that their childhood challenges have inspired them to do the work they do now. They want to make life easier and be there for their students in ways no one was there for them as a child.

We find that more than 85% of the childhood challenges people share with us relate to social identities. Social identities typically infer a hierarchical ranking, so they have more to do with how other people see us than how we see ourselves. In schools and in life, they can be the basis of exclusion.

Three Levels of Identity

We break identity down into three components.

Personal identities are unique and individual. Everyone is different, and constellations of aspects form our identities, and these aspects include interests, talents, personality characteristics, affinities, beliefs, opinions, hobbies, talents, and gifts.

Social identities are group identities. Race, gender, social class, abilities, sexual orientation, religion, language, and cultural background are social identifiers, and these components of identity are not chosen, but rather assigned and determined by the environmental conditions we are born into. Race, for example, has no biological basis other than superficial skin color, but certainly the ways society has constructed the meaning of race has profound effects on our life experiences.

Universal Identities includes qualities valued by almost every culture, such as love, respect, trust, acceptance, forgiveness, and honesty. Universal identities are what people mean when they say we're "all the same." Living out these characteristics, however, depends on recognizing and affirming our personal and social identities.

Sometimes people ask, "But aren't we all human?" This is certainly a true statement. We do all share certain universal human biology and classification, yet we don't all have the same life experiences. When someone insists that all people identify as "human" to the exclusion of any other aspects of their identity, the implication can invalidate life experiences that exert a strong influence on a person's sense of who they are.

When someone identifies as human, and yet also recognizes their social and individual characteristics, they are demonstrating a more advanced awareness of the reciprocal nature of affirmation and identity development. We have to work out our identity issues on personal and social levels in addition to recognizing our universal identities. We need to explore our racial identity conditioning before we can realize our own and other's universal identities. We have to go through race as a part of our identity formation; we can't go around it or skip over it. Moreover, we can't insist on focusing just on universal identity. We need to appreciate the interplay between personal, social, and universal aspects of each individual's identity.

Certain central aspects of a person's identity become more or less important based on the context or environment they are in at the moment. Our students of color frequently describe code switching, or changing their speech, tone, and mannerisms when they enter a white space so that they can gain acceptance. When Dietra presents to a group, she may be more aware and focused on her identity as a Black woman if she's talking with a group of white women. She may be more aware of her hair as a Black woman, especially if it is in a natural hair style, if she's in a room with more Black women, many of whom also have natural hair. The shared experience of natural hair gives her a sense of comfort and connection.

Environment Matters

Our students' identities are formed in a reciprocal relationship with their environments. Their self-concepts are dependent on the (affirmative or not) feedback they get from those they care about and are surrounded by. If the feedback is positive, that aspect of their identity is strengthened. If the feedback is negative, they may adapt and take on a role that allows them to exist and "survive" but not thrive in the environment. If a Black child is expected to be a "performer" in grade school, he may fulfil those expectations instead of becoming a full student who is a performer, learner/scholar, and sensitive caretaker. In elementary school, Daryn attended a predominantly white school.

> I would always be the first one to finish my work, and then because I was bored, I would play around. I was seen as a problem child, and my parents got calls from the school every week. It wasn't until I transferred to another school and had a Black teacher that I was recognized as gifted. She gave me extra challenge work and the phone calls home stopped.

As facilitators, we have the privilege of creating environments where identities can be affirmed, whether it is those of children, our peers, or others we may lead in this work. Creating the environment where individuals find it inviting to bring multiple components of their identities into a space not only matters for them, but it creates a richer environment for everyone and makes our work more rewarding. When we affirm our students' full identities, we empower their agency. As influential others and trusted adults, we can consciously and intentionally design spaces and experiences that strengthen their racial identities.

The danger to avoid is the flattening of identity. As Chimanada Adichie (2009) shares in her highly viewed Ted Talk "The Danger of a Single Story," students need environments that allow them to see a constellation of many stories and for these stories to reflect the many aspects of who they are. They also need room to explore and change how they view those aspects;

they need opportunities not to be the stereotype. Research tells us that the mental health of an individual is at risk when they over identify with a stereotype. For example, the "angry Black woman" stereotype harms young women of color. If they can only be identified as angry, they do not have room to also be joyful, introspective, or fragile. Over identification with stereotypes leads to depression and poor self-esteem (Gordon, 2016). We need to create space for our students and our co-workers to be full people and express the many stories and the many aspects of their identities.

Identity Formation Theory

Identity formation is not just an inside job or a natural process of unfoldment that every human being goes through. Identities, in general, are formed in a reciprocal relationship with their environment. Erikson (1968) believed that certain potentials and limitations are ideally actualized at specific points along the spectrum of human development, and that environmental conditions often facilitate or inhibit their development.

When it comes to racial identity development, there's a much bigger picture. Significantly different sets of circumstances may make up the environments our students find themselves in.

Aspects of Identity

Identity formation theory is backed up by 50 years of research (Crocetti et al., 2007; Evans et al., 2010; Phinney et al., 1997, 2007). As individuals move through stages of identity development, they grapple with understanding who they are and where they belong. Identity exploration is a necessary stage of development if one is to reach adulthood with a solid sense of one's self and one's purpose in the world.

To begin exploring the general concept of identity, we use an activity called "Aspects of Identity." We've used this exercise with children as young as seven years old, and we've used it with C-suite leaders. We ask participants to make a list of ten aspects of their identities, groups that they belong to, or characteristics that define who they are. Nine-year-old Travis listed aspects of his identity as mixed-race, boy, smart, athletic, son, brother, and a gamer. Seven-year-old Shaun listed artist, reader, rock climber, and singer. Dietra listed Black, female, mother of an only child, daughter of an educator, Southern, and oldest child. Each individual's identity is a constellation of many aspects, and these various categories of being all form the story of who we are, each of us as a unique individual.

After participants have listed ten aspects of their identities, we invite them to identify three core aspects of who they are and create a pie chart that shows how important each of the three aspects are to them in their lives.

Next, participants work in small groups to share the story of their pie. How did their pie get formed? Why are each of those aspects of identity meaningful to them? What's the intersection or relationship to how the pie was divided?

When people hear the stories of an individual's pie, they begin to connect with them, and sometimes hearing others' identity stories causes them to rethink their own pie. They begin to see how the environments we are in, particularly during childhood, may highlight or nullify certain important parts of who we are as individuals. Travis's pie, for example, showed that his multiracial identity was the most important aspect of identity for him. The ensuing conversation gave Travis the space to share how central his racial identity is to him. He shared that because he doesn't fall into just one racial category, either Black or white, he sometimes feels that he doesn't fit in anywhere. Learning that Travis felt that way opened the door for more conversation for the educators in his school to think about how to respond to multiracial children, the fastest growing demographic in the nation.

A white participant who shared her pie with a Black woman said,

I was surprised that our pies were basically the same. We both identified as women, Christian, and a mom as central to who we are. But when we shared our pies, I could also see

how I have never thought about my faith as a white woman before. Not until I heard her story and realized how different our stories were.

A Black woman in a session shared,

I have never felt safe to be my full self. Having this session, supported by my administration, gives me hope that they really mean it when they say "bring your full self" into the classroom. In my last job, I could only be part of my true self, and I got really sick and left that school. Of the many different aspects that make up who I am, some are affirmed in the classroom by my students who want to hear my story. When I am my full self, they are able to share more of their stories with the class and be healthy and fully engaged.

In another example, a white woman shared how she was proud of being the "get it done" person. She saw this as an important and positive part of her identity. She knew that at times her drive to "get things done" had created some tension with people of color, but she just saw it as an unchangeable part of her personality. With this activity and exploration of the various components of her identity, she began to see how that characteristic had been affirmed by her culture. She was also encouraged not to see herself as white. She was instead encouraged to see herself as "human" and to focus on her individual unique qualities, such as her flair for creative writing and subsequent educational degree. She began to see how her culture had influenced her identity in ways that had been invisible to her before.

Activities like these help all participants see the interplay between intersecting aspects of identity and better understand how identity development unfolds in a reciprocal relationship with their environments. As teachers, we can create classroom environments that affirm healthy characteristics of a student's identity matrix and reflect back the most promising picture of their emerging self.

The Neurological and Psychological Impact of Racism

Every human being yearns to belong. We are wired to connect. We will find ways to connect, even when we are being harmed by a relationship. According to neuroscientists (Kawamoto, 2017), our brain is genetically coded to protect us. The brain experiences social isolation as danger and as pain. It quickly responds to protect us. When a person experiences social isolation, the same part of the brain is activated as when they experience physical pain (Eisenberger, Lieberman, & Williams, 2003). Students of color experience greater degrees of social isolation than white students. These students are navigating the social pain of outsider-ness.

The saying goes that sticks and stones may break my bones but words will never harm me. The argument can be made that words can hurt us even more deeply and for a longer period of time than physical pain. There are people in their seventies in psychotherapy because of words that were spoken to them in middle and high school. Racial trauma has long term psychological effects that last well into adulthood with symptoms that mimic post-traumatic stress disorder (PTSD), including depression, hypervigilance, anxiety, rumination, anger, and isolation to list only a few (Racism, bias, and discrimination resources, 2021). Without going into depth in this book, it is simply important to know that one of the first steps toward healing racial trauma is to acknowledge that it is real. People need support in developing strong identities, identities that are not stereotypes. And they need environments that support their full selves, where the ability to code switch, for example, is not required for survival.

Why Identity Matters: Three Stages of Development

Identification and learning are inextricably bound. All learning is channeled through the identities our students claim, and it is imperative for educators to understand the profound implications of racial identity on teaching and learning.

Over the years, various scholars have developed charts and grids that describe different stages of identity development for Latinx, Black American, Asian American, Native American, and white racial identity development (Parker & Willsea, 2011). Some models have four, five, or six stages, but we've distilled these into three basic stages: (1) Naïve and Unquestioning; (2) Identity Exploration; and (3) Reintegration and Commitment.

The Hero's Journey outlines the identity quest. The hero begins in a naïve stage of identity development (characteristic of childhood). When her sense of integrity is challenged by an encounter with injustice, she is catapulted into the exploration stage (characteristic of adolescence). She attempts to right the wrong, not only for herself, but also for the good of others. She travels into the underworld where she fights enemies both inside and outside herself. If she prevails, she returns to the world transformed. Her return from the underworld symbolizes the reintegration stage (characteristic of adulthood) where the hero emerges with a sense of higher purpose. She is ready to share the inner gifts she gained on her journey with her community.

Naïve and Unquestioning

Most children believe what their parents believe or tell them is true. They haven't developed a separate sense of themselves as distinct from their parents that allows them to do anything other than uphold the status quo and seek the approval of authority figures. In the naive stage, assumptions are unquestioned and mindsets are unexamined.

For marginalized groups, the naïve stage can result in internalizing negative stereotypes or believing the stereotypes about their group are true. A Black student in the naive stage may believe she doesn't belong in an advanced placement class. "There's this false narrative about Black people's intelligence and white kids think that you got in with lower stats than they did," says Korrie. "At first it affected me and I struggled with imposter syndrome, I felt like I didn't deserve to be there."

A white student in the naive stage may harbor racial bias. She may have seen and heard negative messages about other racial groups so many times that she believes they're true. And if nothing in her life challenges her assumptions, she will continue to believe them.

Exploration

Something usually happens to catapult an individual into the identity exploration phase. It's often an encounter with injustice, but it can also be a more gradual recognition of injustices. The exploration stage is described as an "identity crisis" by Erikson (1968) as it's almost always emotional. Waking up to injustice is painful. High emotions like confusion, anger, and sadness are characteristic of the exploration stage. These emotions, however, provide fuel for growth. The exploration phase is guided by a drive to resolve inner conflict and make sense of unfairness.

Effects on Students of Color

In our society, people of color, in general, leave the naive stage of racial identity development and enter the exploration stage earlier than white people. If children of color haven't encountered racism by the time they start school, their parents necessarily have to prepare them for it.

Most children of color do, in fact, encounter racism at school. They are far more likely than white children to encounter teachers who underestimate their intelligence, expect less of them, and discipline them more often. A Yale study (Hathaway, 2016) showed that even in preschool, teachers watch black boys three times more than other children, anticipating discipline infractions.

For students of color, there's a need for same-identity rela-tionships for comfort, nurturing, and mirroring during the explo-ration phase. At the height of exploration, they may need to focus entirely on same identity relationships at least temporarily for additional support and understanding. Those connections are always going to be necessary, although they may not always be exclusive. Academic inquiry into their group's history and heritage can help mitigate some of the emotional intensity.

Effects on White Students

White children, on the other hand, may not enter the explora-tion phase of racial identity development until much later, if at all. It's not uncommon for white adults to be in a naïve stage of racial identity. Some white adults deny that they have a racial identity. "I don't think of myself as white," they say, "I just think of myself as human." Problems occur when people don't grow out of the naïve stage, and Kohlberg's (1976) research on moral development showed that a lot of people don't. He believed a large majority of adults avoid the struggle of identity exploration and stay at a conventional level, never reaching higher orders of critical thinking and moral reasoning.

Coming to realize that you're a member of an oppressor group begins an intense process of self-examination that can result in feelings of confusion, guilt, anger, and shame. In the early stages of exploration, white people may identify in oppo-sition to the dominant group and say, "I'm not like other white people." They may also feel an urgency to "fix" racism. They desperately want to "do something." Yet until they process their own emotions and learn to listen to the voices of people of color, they have difficulty working in equal partnerships to address the impact of racism. They may come across as a "white savior," and in their "rush to fix" racism, they tend to reproduce it. They need models of white allies and advocates to help them distin-guish themselves as white co-liberators. It may help them to recognize that whiteness is an ideology, but white racial identity connotes a skin color. And many, many people with white skin care deeply about ending racism. There is a rich legacy of white race activists for them to identify with.

Reintegration, Commitment, and Community

The result of identity exploration is reintegration. A person comes out of exploration with a multidimensional sense of self and a more fluid identity. In this stage, a person has a firm foundation for who they are and is empowered to identify the contributions they have to offer. The reintegration phase is associated with increased psychological health, self-esteem, and confidence.

In the reintegration phase, a person can think critically, see multiple perspectives, and hold space for differences. They become more aware of their own boundaries which makes them more sensitive to and respectful of the boundaries that are important to others. This heightened self-awareness helps build safer communities in which people of different identities can coexist.

This stage is characterized by a commitment to a higher cause, which is why we associate identity exploration and reintegration with ethical leadership. Educators, in particular, are frequently motivated by the desire to serve a higher purpose. They strive to make a contribution to the well-being of the next generation and to leave the world a better place than they found it. Their commitment aligns with building a sense of shared community in which everyone is invited to share their authentic voice.

Individuals in the reintegration stage are inspired to take action to bring about equitable change. By the time they reach this stage, they have developed patience and have cultivated a strategic mindset that allows time for processing, listening to the voices of the people most impacted by racism, and collaborating across differences to transform their environment.

A student of color who progresses through the exploration phase to the achievement stage necessarily learns to protect their sense of integrity. This is no small feat. Like the hero's journey, it requires fighting enemies both within and without. They learn not to believe the stereotypes, to deflect negative projections, to navigate microaggressions, and to find a stable core within. They manage to maintain their sense of self-worth even in the face of routine psychological assault.

Benefits of Identity Exploration and Achievement

When people dive into identity exploration, they have the opportunity to reflect on all things past and present that have influenced and shaped the formation of who they are. For example, when reflecting on an experience with injustice, a student might encounter pain points when sharing what transpired. However, there is liberty in sharing how those painful encounters have transformed and empowered them to become the person they are.

Fifty years of research in identity formation (Crocetti et al., 2007; Evans et al, 2010; Phinney et al., 1997, 2007;) demonstrates a host of benefits of identity exploration: higher engagement in school, better social skills, increased academic performance, critical thinking, more resilience and a greater sense of connectedness. Besides that, kids are already exploring their identities. Identity formation is a normal and natural process. In most cases, they're just doing it on their own, separate from what they do in school.

Dimensions of Leadership in Identity Formation Learning

The identity quest is driven by a desire to be a good person and to be part of a good people. Erikson (1968) says, "An ethical capacity is the true criteria of identity." Kohlberg (1976) believed only a minority of people make it into the post-conventional stage of moral reasoning, which is associated with identity reintegration and commitment. Our hope is that if educators can support identity formation, more people can reach a higher potential and more people will emerge as leaders in the movement toward equitable change.

References

Adichie, C. N. (2009). The danger of a single story. *TED Talks*. Retrieved from https://www.youtube.com/watch?v=D9Ihs241zeg

American Psychological Association. (2021). *Racism, bias, and discrimination resources*. American Psychological Association. Retrieved from https://www.apa.org/topics/racism-bias-discrimination

Crocetti, E., Rubini, M., Luyckx, K. & Meeus, W. H. (2007). Identity formation in early and middle adolescents from various ethnic groups: From three dimensions to five statuses. *Journal of Youth and Adolescence, 37*(8), 983–996.

Eisenberger, N. I., Lieberman, M. D. & Williams, K. D. (2003). Does rejection hurt? An fMRI study of social exclusion. *Science, 302*, 290–292. doi:10.1126/science.1089134

Erikson, E. H. (1968). *Identity: Youth and crisis*. New York: Norton.

Evans, N. J., Foreney, D. S., Guido, F. M., Patton, L. D. & Renn, K. A. (2010). *Student development in college: Theory, research, and practice* (2nd Ed.). San Francisco, CA: John Wiley & Sons.

Gordon, D. (2016, Jan 13). Discrimination can be harmful to your health. *UCLA Newsroom*.

Hathaway, B. (2016, Sep 27). Implicit bias may help explain high preschool expulsion rates for Black children. Yale News. Retrieved from https://news.yale.edu/2016/09/27/implicit-bias-may-explain-high-preschool-expulsion-rates-black-children

Kawamoto, T. (2017). What happens in your mind and brain when you are excluded from a social activity?. *Frontiers for Young Minds, 5*, 46. doi 10.3389/frym.2017.00046

Kohlberg, L. (1976). Moral stages and moralization. In T. Lickona (Ed.), *Moral development and behavior* (pp. 31–53). New York: Holt, Reinhart & Winston.

Parker, C. S. & Willsea, J. (2011). *Summary of stages of racial identity development*. Interaction Institute for Social Change. Retrieved from https://drive.google.com/file/d/1oO42QQhHL6JZanPI9KNOA5iQmtPBAa7O/view

Phinney, J. S., Cantu, C. L. & Kurtz, D. A. (1997). Ethnic and American identity as predictors of self-esteem among African American,

Latino, and White adolescents. *Journal of Youth and Adolescence,* *26*(2), 165–185.

Phinney, J. S. & Ong, A. D. (2007). Conceptualization and measurement of ethnic identity: Current status and future directions. *Journal of Counseling Psychology, 54*(3), 271–281.

3

Cultivating Language to Talk about Race

Danielle was in her ninth-grade history class when Mr Cross, her white teacher, introduced the topic of African American history. As the only Black student in the class, she braced herself for the uncomfortable discussions about slavery that were sure to come since that seemed to be only thing her white teachers knew about Black history. What she was not prepared for, however, was when Mr Cross began to talk about how Black people in the present typically end up in jail, in poverty, and in other unfortunate circumstances.

Danielle understood that Mr Cross was both ignorant and that his ideas were racist, but she didn't want to confront him in class. When class ended, she went straight to the principal's office. "Why don't you ask Mr Cross if you can talk to him outside of class?" the principal advised, "Let him know how you feel about what he said."

When Danielle met with Mr Cross, instead of acknowledging her feelings, he defended his position. "I'm just stating statistical facts," he argued.

"Well, I'm Black, and I've never been to jail and neither has anyone in my family," she explained. She came away with the understanding that what Mr Cross taught his class was what he himself believed. Mr

DOI: 10.4324/9781003191353-4

Cross saw Black people as oppressed and downtrodden. He did not see them as a people who despite having experienced oppression, had resisted oppression every step of the way, and who had surmounted incredible odds not only to survive but lead a movement toward human liberation.

Danielle, the only Black student in the class, was called upon by an administrator to defend herself against the narrow perspectives of a white teacher. Like many students of color in predominantly white schools, she found herself in the position of a student teaching a teacher. She had to be the one to inform him that there was more to Black history than the stories he taught. She later learned that hers was not an isolated incident, but that other Black students had similar experiences in Mr Cross's class over a period of many years.

Talking about race and racism are not the same thing, and before we talk about the forms racial oppression can take, we have to address the need for balance in our curriculum. When we talk about race in school, we have to talk about more than just racism and the oppression of people of color. That people of color have been oppressed is indisputable, but there is so much more to the story. There is a rich and compelling history of accomplishment and contribution to humankind. As well, there are many racial identity groups and a wide diversity of experiences within racial groups. We can't paint the picture with too broad a brush.

A white teacher who focuses primarily on stories of oppression and suffering must explore their own understanding and knowledge of people of color. Facilitators and educators need to balance the stories of the pain with the stories of power, stories of remarkable people who have risen above racism. Ask yourself how you can celebrate the genius in your students who have defied the odds despite what history and society portrays.

José, who teaches five and six-year-olds about the Civil Rights Movement, says, "I teach my students about resistance, not oppression. I want them to recognize what Black Americans have overcome, how much they have accomplished." Before he talks with his students about race, he engages them in a role-playing game in which the children pretend there has been an alien invasion, and they must come up with ways to resist the takeover. Then, when he moves on to introduce stories about change makers and activists from the Civil Rights Movement, his students readily identify with the heroic figures who strategically resisted oppression and built a movement for change.

Facilitating conversations about race requires that we view our work through an "equity lens," and to do so, we need to understand the deep historical and systemic roots of racism. As Tameka, a high school senior, so aptly put it:

> Even if we're advocating for equity, we have to be realistic. That's not the way it is. There are a lot of structures that keep people of color down. Until Black wealth is equal to white wealth, it's not an equal society. It's important for us to have spaces to cope with the hurt that inequality causes. It's important to understand that kids may not even know what they're missing because being isolated and thinking they are the only one who is experiencing trauma is normal for them.

It's important to provide a balanced narrative that includes a study of racial oppression, but not one that is dominated by it. A curriculum that includes conversations about race should be part of a larger narrative about resistance that highlights the strengths and contributions of people of color.

Finding out Who Is in the Room

As facilitators, our job is to invite multiple aspects of our students' identities into our classrooms, to provide opportunities and make spaces for them to share their authentic selves and learn more about the authentic selves of others. We need an approach that recognizes and uplifts their racial identities, yet also includes their gender, social class, family and cultural backgrounds, their linguistic codes and styles of speech, their academic abilities, their emotional temperament, whether they are extroverts or introverts, and other aspects of their identities that make up the complex constellation of who they are.

Aija, an early care curriculum specialist, uses the *Family Culture Survey* to learn more about the lives of her preschool students. (Larry, 2021). She asks children's caregivers about the race, ethnic, and cultural identities of parents, grandparents, and other important people in their lives. She finds out about the traditions and holidays they celebrate; the language(s) they speak at home; how caregivers talk about inclusivity with them; and what they would like for their child to learn about inclusivity, anti-bias, and other cultures. The survey gives her a window into her students' lives outside of school and helps her plan a curriculum that reflects their identities and draws on their backgrounds. Her survey also lets families know that honoring her students' cultural identities and emphasizing inclusivity are important components of her school's curriculum.

Taking an Intersectional Approach

As facilitators, we must be on the cutting edge of identity development, and intersectional work is the next phase of truly inclusive classrooms (Frame, 2021). We must be able to listen and learn from others who see the world differently than we do. The ways we see our students impact how they see themselves, how they relate to school, and how well they learn. Our affinity bias typically works toward our acceptance of students we share common experiences with, and our confirmation bias allows them to connect with us when they see parts of themselves in us. Multiple aspects of their identities are constantly playing out in our classrooms, and we can include multiple aspects of their identities in the methods and materials we use (Frame, 2021).

An intersectional approach can be applied in every discipline and across grades levels and academic abilities. Students rise to academic challenges when their need to be recognized and affirmed is met. By bringing multiple aspects of their identities into our classrooms, we engage the whole child. We learn more about our students and more about how they learn.

Getting to know our students, educating ourselves on how the world sees them versus how they see themselves, takes time. The time invested upfront, however, yields far more in learning and academic advances later down the line. Bobby, a teacher in Atlanta Public Schools, offers "Talk about it Tuesdays" for his ninth-grade students. He sets aside regular class time for them to talk about their lives outside of school. They share their interests and concerns, and how they are feeling about stories in the news. They talk about family events and what they are learning in other classes. "It helps me keep my finger on the pulse of what's going with them, and it strengthens their relationships with each other," says Bobby. "Rather than taking time away from learning, they do better in school because of these conversations."

The future of learning is an equal and inclusive space, a place for students to open up and be vulnerable about their identities, to bring their whole selves into the room rather than leave parts of who they are at the door. When we recognize the complexities and gifts of our students, we unlock the doors between them by just allowing them to be present for each other's realities. We create spaces of belonging where it is important to listen and learn, as well as to express and exist. In doing this, they end up sharing each other's pain, and healing through mutual understanding (Frame, 2021).

Starting with Race

Identity is a multiplicity of components, but when we talk to students, teachers, and other professionals about equity and inclusion, we start with the topic of race. Omi and Winant (2015) call race a "master category" of oppression and view it as a "fundamental organizing principle of injustice in the U. S." Race has provided a template for the subordination of other groups. Yet the continuous resistance of Black people has also provided a template for liberation. From the Harlem Renaissance to Black Wall Street to the Civil Rights Movement to Black Lives Matter, the Black Movement has led the nation toward liberation.

The impact of race is pervasive and touches every aspect of our lives. As the struggle for racial justice moves to the forefront of the public imagination, the connections between historical causes and current issues are more apparent now than ever. A study of race offers a rich history of resistance, most of which is still absent from school curricula. Race offers abundant texts and resources for academic inquiry, problem based learning, and participatory action projects.

Because racism has served as a master category of oppression, and because it offers us a template for liberation, we believe focusing our collective intelligence on alleviating the suffering racism has caused and continues to cause will benefit us all. Now is the time for us to work together to cultivate a new vision of a multiracial society.

By establishing language around identity, we can create learning experiences that center race, yet includes other components of identity. In an intersectional approach, race provides an overarching theme that allows for the examination of race, as well as other aspects of identity that intersect with race. A student who is woman of color, for example, needs a narrative that affirms both her race and her gender. In a literature class reading Chimamanda Ngozi Adiche's *Purple Hibiscus*, students might explore how Kambili's character is influenced by the legacy of colonialism in Nigeria. Her race, gender, social status, and religious identities all intersect and are crucial to how her story plays out. A history class might be centered on race, but could reflect on gender as a tertiary intersecting identity. In the struggle for women's rights, for instance, racial power dynamics between Black, Latina, Asian, and Indigenous women and white women not only merit historical analysis, but the recognition that these dynamics continue to play out in feminist studies today. An intersectional focus allows teachers and students to understand that racial identities have layered aspects, and racism has different impacts on different social groups.

Calculating the Cognitive Cost of Racism

We ask people in our workshops to weigh how important their racial identities are to them on a scale of 1 to 10. For example: How often are you aware of your race during a normal day, and how much of your attention is consumed by this awareness? White people usually rate their weight between 1 and 3, while people of color give their racial identities a weight of between 7 and 9. This discrepancy is an important delineation. Wherever an identity aspect is marginalized, like race, it takes up more of a person's attention and consumes more space in their consciousness. Mental and emotional energy is diverted from daily tasks. This difference in how a person experiences their racial identity on a day-to-day basis is important to be aware of when you're facilitating conversations that engage encounters involving students' lived experience. Students of color are typically more aware of their race, so they may have more to share, but they may also need protection so that they do not feel overburdened. As white students cultivate empathy and race awareness, they begin to share some of the cognitive load.

"How much does your identity weigh?" is a deceptively simple and yet profound question. People of color may not realize and may not initially share how much energy they divert into thinking about, planning around, and anticipating how they will navigate their day. A Black teacher shared a story about a trip with his soon to be father-in-law to a neighboring town to get legal papers for his upcoming wedding. He reduced his cruising speed to below the speed limit, removed his hat, earring, and sunglasses as they entered the town. On reflection, he shared with the group that every day he reviews where he will need to travel that day to determine what clothes he will wear to reduce the chances of being noticed and seen as threatening. After hearing this story, a Black woman shared her intentional approach to the hair styles she wears, indicating her preference to wear a natural hair style, but defaulting to a straight perm during the school year to reduce questions and commentary by her co-workers. She noted that she loves having her students inquire about her hair because she feels like their questions are genuine, and she knows they are not judging her. Her co-workers' questions, however, sometimes feel intrusive and judgmental.

As teachers describe the role their racial identities play in their lives, they learn from each other. White teachers note that in their day-to-day life, they are not making adjustments or thinking about their race during outings with family, while shopping, or driving. If they do think of their race, it is not in the context of needing a sense of protection like many Black, Indigenous, and people of color mention in the stories they share. Some white teachers experience a heightened awareness of their race when they teach in predominantly Black schools. Their students ask questions about their race, and sometimes challenge them.

Speaking Truth to Transform the World

Human beings long to make a mark on the world, and language is the medium through which we enact change. Friere (1970, p. 87) said "to speak a true word is to transform the world." He believed language is the key to transformational change. Language opens windows into our past and releases our ideas about our potential future, allowing us to make informed choices in the present. "The inherent capacity for language to enact transformation can be harnessed through dialogue, one of the most powerful resources in the critical educator's toolkit," says Mischnick (2021). "All meaningful conversations are linked to actions that matter, actions that transform the world. Dialogue discusses the current reality with the aim of changing it."

Conversations about race build language, understanding, and knowledge through a collective quest. When parties are working from a shared vision of an inclusive human family, they feel safe enough to be brave enough to share their authentic perspectives because they know their voices will be heard and that their conversations will produce action that matters. We learn from the rich knowledge of the people around us and as a result, all of our perspectives are broadened.

Defining Levels of Racism

Leading conversations about racial experience requires us to confront racial inequities on multiple levels, including interpersonal, internal, intra-group, and institutional levels. These concepts are discussed in more detail in *Let's Get Real: Exploring Race, Class, and Gender Identities in the Classroom* (Caldwell & Frame, 2022).

Developing a common language to talk about race and racism helps students develop a more nuanced view of how racism operates in their lives and in society. When they share a common language for conversations about race, they can move into deeper levels of understanding and application. As you facilitate conversations about race, you will find these terms useful in your work. Your students may identify how some of these concepts are playing out in their experience or in power dynamics in the school. These deeper conversations help them explore ways to understand not only how they are personally impacted by race, racism, and racial identities, but also help them develop strategies to counteract racism.

We introduce four categories of racism that describe how racial oppression operates on multiple levels in the lives of both privileged and marginalized identities. These categories can be applied to any social identity because they operate in both socially advantaged and marginalized groups. For our purposes, however, we will be applying these definitions to race, racism, and racial identities.

Level 1: Interpersonal racism occurs between individuals. Because so many people still view racism as individual acts of discrimination, and because they don't personally use racial slurs or willfully exclude people of color, they may initially feel defensive in conversations about race. "Why are white people always the bad guys?" we sometimes hear. To understand the impact of racism, students must expand their definitions of racism beyond the interpersonal level.

Unconscious bias can be a form of interpersonal racism because it's often acted out between individuals. Unconscious bias involves unexamined assumptions and attitudes that operate below the level of awareness. It occurs when someone has been conditioned to believe that negative stereotypes are true, and they haven't yet developed the cognitive mechanisms to question and then counteract these assumptions.

Microaggressions are subtle forms of undermining that people of color experience on a routine basis in their day-to-day experience. Microaggressions include everyday slights, putdowns, insults, and sometimes even compliments that undermine a person's sense of identity and confidence. Microaggressions can be unintentional and are sometimes even well meaning, but their frequency over time has a cumulative impact. They create confusion, anxiety, depression, diminished self-confidence, and can result in disengagement from school.

Level 2: Internalized Racism describes the psychological internalization of unexamined assumptions, prejudices, and stereotypical beliefs about oneself and one's own group. Racism is internalized when stereotypes are so relentlessly projected onto people of color until they become internalized in their consciousness and, in effect, are believed to be true.

W. E. B. Dubois describes *double consciousness* as the experience Black people have when they're required to see themselves through the lens of a white supremacist society (Dubois, 1897). In one part of their minds, they have to recognize how they're seen by society because they have to negotiate that society in order to function and survive within it. Yet in order to thrive, they must also remain aware of their own humanity, intelligence, and integrity.

Claude Steele (Steele, 2011a, 2011b) studied a variety of identity groups to establish the prevalence of *stereotype threat*. His research gives insight into just how damaging oppression can be on cognition and learning. Stereotype threat happens when an individual feels threatened by a negative stereotype about their group and are afraid that they will confirm it. The anxiety the threat produces inhibits mental processing and interferes with academic performance. Steele found that stereotype threat inhibited cognition in Black students when they were told before taking a test that Black students typically score lower than white students on it. Like a self-fulfilling prophecy, Black students did indeed score lower than white students on the test. However, when Black students were primed before the test by hearing that Black students typically score just as well as white students on the test, they scored slightly higher than white students. Steele also found that white people experience stereotype threat when they fear confirming the stereotype that white people are racist.

White Privilege can also be internalized. The term refers to the accumulation of unearned rights, benefits, and social status markers conferred through unequal financial and educational opportunities granted to white individuals through consecutive generations. Internalized privilege may be based on a person's unconscious attitudes about the assumed superiority of their own racial group and can be expressed as a denial that racism exists or as paternalism. It results in obliviousness to other people's experience, lack of empathy, and ultimately, poor decision-making based on "not knowing what you don't know." In classrooms, it manifests in the prevalence of Eurocentric curriculum, the deficit narrative about students of color, and in the continued perpetration of microaggressions and stereotype threat on students of color.

Level 3: Intra-group Racism manifests when people in marginalized groups internalize negative beliefs about themselves and seek to conform and assimilate to dominant white cultural standards. This can result in the denial of oppression's effects, distancing oneself from one's own group, victim blaming, and transmitting oppressive norms to children.

Level 4: Institutionalized/Systemic Racism refers to the ways exclusion and mistreatment of people of color has been supported and enforced through social institutions and systems of law that have affected opportunities for education, housing, employment, and wealth-building. The way out of the limiting mindsets of interpersonal, internalized, and intra-group racism is to understand institutional or systemic racism. To understand why racial disparities continue to exist, we have to understand how social systems have historically disadvantaged people of color.

Conclusion

In facilitating conversations about race, racism, and racial identities, it's most important to take a strength-based approach. Knowing your students as individual, unique beings and considering their intersecting identities fosters a sense of belonging in the classroom. Educators who understand the cognitive impact of the disproportionate awareness of race, racism, and racial identity in the minds of students of color can help mitigate its effects. Cultivating a shared vocabulary to talk about racism gives students language to describe their experience and broadens their definition of racism beyond interpersonal racism to include an understanding of systemic racism. In Martha's eighth grade class, students quickly grasped these terms. They had all experienced or witnessed racism, and given a language to describe it, they put it to use immediately. Students of color could identify how internalized racism had affected their self-confidence and how stereotype threat had limited their potential. White students could see how racial privilege had kept them oblivious to disparities and blinded them to reality. They understood how racism kept them separated and interfered with their capacity to form trusting relationships with each other.

Paul Gorski (2021) advises educators to "prioritize the interests of the students and families whose interests historically have not been prioritized," and to ask themselves, "What impact is this going to have on the most marginalized students and families?" We counteract the effects of racism by centering the educational experiences of students of color, by amplifying their voices, and listening and learning from and about the students most impacted by racism. Our classrooms and curricula can shift the narrative about race when we emphasize the contributions of communities of color, and highlight resistance, resilience, and triumph.

References

Caldwell, M. & O. Frame (2022). *Let's get real: Exploring race, class, and gender identities in the classroom.* New York: Routledge.

Dubois, W. E. B. (1897, Aug). Strivings of the Negro people. *Atlantic Monthly.* Retrieved from www.theatlantic.com/past/unbound/flashbks/black/dubstriv.htm

Frame, O. (2021). An intersection in our educational lives: We are more than meets the eye. In J. Casas, O. L. Mayers, and J. Zoul (Eds.) *10 Perspectives on Equity in Education.* (68–79) New York: Routledge.

Friere, P. (1970). *Pedagogy of the oppressed.* New York: The Seabury Press.

Gorski, P. (2021). Basic principles of equity literacy. Equity Literacy Institute. Retrieved from https://www.equityliteracy.org/equity-principles

Larry, A. (2021). Family culture survey. Tryadic Education. Retrieved from https://tryadiceducation.org

Mischnick, S. (2021, Jul 6). Blossom as an educator: Cultivate your craft and flourish with critical pedagogy. Miss Adventure in the Classroom. Retrieved from https://www.missadventureintheclassroom.com/post/blossom-as-an-educator

Omi, M. & Winant, H. (2015). *Racial formations in the United States* (3rd Ed.). New York: Routledge. NAACP (2015).

Steele, C. (2011a). *Whistling Vivaldi: How stereotypes affect us and what we can do.* New York: W. W. Norton & Company.

Steele, C. (2011b). Stereotype threat and African-American student achievement. In D. Gruskey's & Szelenyi (Eds.), *Inequality reader: Contemporary and foundational readings in race, class, and gender.* (276–281) Boulder, CO: Westview Press.

4

Learning from Students' Stories

Luis was one of a handful of Latinx students at his school. During his junior year, while on his way to class, Luis passed Mr Farnsworth, the school principal. Mr Farnsworth smiled broadly and extended his hand. In very deliberate and slow English, Mr Farnsworth said, "Welcome to America and welcome to our school!" Luis timidly shook the white principal's hand. Luis had been a student at the school since third grade.

The school was hosting a special event that day. Brazilian students were visiting campus as part of an exchange program, and Mr Farnsworth had mistaken Luis for one of the international exchange students.

Luis shared his story with a group of educators at the iChange Collaborative Race Institute for Educators. He and several other students of color gathered to share their school experiences with the educators in attendance. The teachers, counselors, and administrators leaned in to listen, spellbound by the students' compelling, sometimes heartbreaking stories.

The student panels at our institutes provide spaces for students of color to be seen, heard, and appreciated. We strategically ensure a healing space for these students and a learning space for educators who want to get it right. In an environment of mutual

DOI: 10.4324/9781003191353-5

respect and appreciation, these educators have the opportunity to listen and learn from the people most impacted by the dynamics of race in education, students of color. The students are more than willing to take advantage of this platform because the invitation to be transparent has often not been extended by their schools or by society. They show up because they want educators to understand their experience in school, and they appreciate the educators for listening to them. "I can't tell you how much it means that you want to learn about my experience," Jovan told the educators. Bettina echoed his response, "I had been thinking that somehow my contributions to this world may be undervalued or underappreciated. Today I was heard, accepted, appreciated, and thanked. I really needed the encouragement to know that it all matters to someone."

These facilitated conversations offer safe and brave spaces for both teachers and students of color to interact, transfer invaluable information, and practice appreciative communication methods. The student panel demonstrates the power of listening to student voices and positions teachers to begin these conversations in their own spaces.

Facilitating a student panel can be challenging, however, because the expectation is that the students will provide insight for the educators. Yet their insights usually come from experiences of pain and sometimes trauma. Balancing the needs of educators who benefit from having access to the students' stories with the students' need for emotional support calls for a deliberate strength-based approach. It means inviting students of color not only to share their stories of marginalization but also to share their stories of accomplishment, appreciation for their educational experiences, and who they are as individuals.

Our panel facilitation method comes from Danielle's research on the self-esteem of students of color in predominantly white institutions. She begins by interviewing each student participant individually to get to know them, discuss their experiences and insights, and give them background about the institute. Then she connects them with each other in a "meet and greet" session prior to their participation on the panel. They naturally form connections based on their shared experiences, and these connections provide peer support for them when they share their stories with the educators. Meeting together before the panel discussion reassures them that they are not alone.

Stories from Students of Color

In a safe and brave environment, students of color frequently take the lead in conversations about race, telling personal stories about what it's like to be stereotyped or how it feels to be looked at with suspicion when they haven't done anything wrong. They describe microaggressions and incidents that leave them wondering if race played a role in a weird interaction. Because of their background knowledge, they emerge as experts and leaders in these conversations. Their white peers are fascinated by their stories because, so often, they weren't aware of how their classmates of color were experiencing racism.

Students of color feel the weight of their racial identity when they are faced with perceptions about them that don't match their sense of who they are. As facilitators we must understand the prevalence of the assumptions, the stereotypes, the microaggressions, and other forms of racism they routinely encounter so that we can protect them, teach them, and help them counteract the impact of racism in their lives. Until we do, these patterns of racial experience will continue to interfere with our capacity to build trust with students.

Students of color frequently talk about *code switching*, or changing their behavior, language, and mannerisms when they're at school. Because they don't feel their home cultural style would be accepted at school, they may act one way at home, in their neighborhoods and communities, and another way at school. Fifteen-year-old Micah shares:

I live in a predominantly Black area, but I go to a white school. My Black friends ask me why I talk so 'proper,' and my white friends assume I talk 'slang.' The white kids change the way they talk around me and greet me with a 'Yo, what up, bruh?'

And then ask, 'Did I say it right?' But they talk to other white kids in a regular tone. I'm not trying to talk Black or white, I'm just speaking like me. Why do I have to sound like I'm white to sound intelligent? And what does that even mean? I realized it's just easier for me to code switch to make everyone happy. I try to sound a little more 'ethnic' with my Black friends and 'white' with my white friends. It's just easier that way for everyone else.

Students of color also describe incidents in which they encountered racially charged language and slurs.

I was with a group of white friends from school at a house party. We were all dancing and then the music changed to Jay-Z's N- What, N- Who, and the crowd started singing along, yelling the lyrics. I walked off feeling really uncomfortable. As I was walking away, one of my friends said 'What's up, n-?'

Black students routinely hear white students use the n-word and describe things as "ghetto" or "gangster." They feel extremely uncomfortable when their white peers use racialized language, even if the intent is to be humorous. Their peers underestimate the pain they feel hearing jokes or comments about race. Students of color don't know how to respond or who they can go to for help.

Unfortunately, students of color also describe instances of hearing the n-word used in the classroom. Lawrence described hearing his white teacher and white peers use the n-word in class discussions of *To Kill a Mockingbird*.

Every time someone said that word, I cringed, and it felt like everyone was looking at me. When I talked to the teacher about it, her explanation was that it was a part of the text. She never acknowledged my feelings and never checked in with me after that. To this day, all I remember about that book is how it felt when people said that word.

Students of color tell us it's not uncommon for them to be viewed with suspicion or seen as threatening in encounters both inside and outside of school. They expect to be disciplined more harshly and know they can't get away with some of the behaviors their white classmates can. Almost every student of color we've heard from reports at least one incident of being questioned by security guards or followed by store clerks while shopping. "My boyfriend came to pick me up from my private school early," says Victoria, a Latinx student.

> *My boyfriend came to pick me up from my private school early, says Victoria, a Latinx student, shares: While he was sitting in his car, he saw a security officer coming towards him, so he drove away. When I came outside, I heard people talking, and when I asked what was going on, someone said that security had just scared off a Hispanic who was parked in front of the school. Another kid said they heard he had a gun and was trying to rob someone. I didn't realize who they were talking about was my boyfriend. When security caught him and asked him why he was on campus he told them that he was picking up his girlfriend. Security then questioned me about why my boyfriend was there to pick me up."*

Students of color understand that they are stereotyped as potential shoplifters, thieves, and troublemakers, especially if they are in a group. Some report having their backpacks searched unnecessarily. Others talk about being accused of cheating when they turn in excellent work.

Students of color frequently describe their experiences with white teachers and college counselors who underestimate their level of intelligence and academic potential. "I wish that all of my teachers and counselors would see my full potential and would push me to aim high, but I keep being told that I'm being unrealistic about my goals. My white guidance counselor wanted me to share my future plans, so I opened up and shared them," Marcus explains;

> *"I wish that all of my teachers and counselors would see my full potential and would push me to aim high, but I keep being told that I'm being unrealistic about my goals. My white guidance counselor wanted me to share my future plans, so*

I opened up and shared them." I was traumatized when she told me I would not be a good fit for the schools I wanted to go to. When I told my parents, they decided that I no longer need the support of my guidance counselor, that I just need to apply to the schools they knew I would be able to get into, and we could prove that guidance counselor wrong.

Marcus never told his counselor how he felt or what his parents advised him to do, but he did make a point to show her his acceptance letters.

Especially in predominantly white schools, students of color are not always provided the opportunity to just be students. Even more devastating, Black, Indigenous, and students of color report that they have few opportunities to find support from teachers or staff who understand their experiences. Their teachers of color were often the only ones they felt comfortable talking to about their racial experience, and many of them had few teachers of color. Samara described her support group as consisting of just one teacher. "It wasn't just me, though," she said. "All the Black kids were in her room before school and at lunch." This story resonates with the experience of teachers of color at the institute. They often provide spaces where students of color feel safe. One teacher described her role as a Black teacher at her independent school as an "extra part time job I don't get paid for."

Some students of color, however, report that white teachers have offered them an enormous amount of support. As Kevin says:

"My history teacher was a great source of support for me." She filled in the gaps in her curriculum and did her best to tell the whole story. Not just for Black history, but for other racial groups as well. I'd go sit in her classroom and talk to her at lunch. Those conversations outside of class made a huge difference. I wanted to do well in her class because I knew she cared about me, and I didn't want to let her down.

We hear testimonies of students of color who tell us their racial identities have been reinforced and strengthened by their families and communities. They have been taught to be proud of who they are and where they come from. What they know about Black history and culture, they often learned at home rather than at school. Rhonda shared that she grew up learning about Black history at home.

I sometimes had to write an essay on Black history before I could go outside and play with my friends. We visited Black museums when we traveled. I learned the Black National Anthem. I was surrounded by Black churches, Black teachers, and Black doctors. It takes a village to raise a child, and I had that village from day one.

Students of color have learned to be aware of their racial identity and navigate a society in which they can expect to be racially stereotyped. In some cases, their parents have warned them to be careful around white people (including teachers) and have prepared them for encounters with discrimination. "My parents told me I was at that school to get an education and an experience," says Danielle. "As a young Black woman, I did not necessarily fit in at my white school entirely, but I did what so many other Black students did, I kept my focus on learning."

Black and Brown students who cannot get the support that they need on campus often do not feel completely connected to the school community. Although racial experiences can be quite difficult for these students, they find a sense of support through connections outside of school. While conducting research for her dissertation, *Former Minority Students Perceptions of Self Esteem from Atlanta K-12 Private School Experience*, Danielle (Stewart, 2014) randomly surveyed over 100 alumni of color about performance self-esteem, social self-esteem, appearance self-esteem, and overall self-esteem, using the State Self-Esteem Scale Instrument. Her research revealed that external support from family, mentors, and other people of color who understood the culture of a predominantly white setting nurtured students' self-esteem. These students of color did not lack self-esteem. They did, however, lack support from their school communities, and finding support outside of school was an essential part of how they were able to thrive and made a huge difference in their lives.

Stories from White Students

While students of color are navigating racism at school, white students are having a very different experience. The cost of racism to white people in no way compares to the damage inflicted for hundreds of years on people of color, yet Paulo Friere (1970) reminds us in *Pedagogy of the Oppressed* that oppression dehumanizes both the oppressed and the oppressor. For white educators and white students, understanding the impact of racism on people of color as well as its impact on white people is a necessary step for healing.

In the naive stage of identity development, white identity remains unquestioned. "I don't see myself as white," Harvey says. "I just see myself as human." Harvey hasn't thought much about race because he hasn't faced challenges to his racial identity. Like many white students, he doesn't see race as a meaningful component of his identity or associate it with his culture, history, and ideology. He has lived his life so far, oblivious to the reality that people of color are having very different life experiences than he is.

Because white students typically "haven't had to know" that racism exists, they frequently enter these conversations in a naïve stage of racial identity development. "I thought racism went out with the Civil Rights Movement," said 13-year-old Trish, after hearing her friend Akhil and other students of color describe being followed by store clerks while shopping. "I've known Akhil since elementary school, and I'm shocked to learn that he's been dealing with this."

White students' responses to learning that racism is alive and well and playing itself out in the lives of their friends can be emotional. They may initially feel confused, defensive, guilty, or ashamed of their prior ignorance. "How could I not have known this?" Karina wrote after hearing her classmates of color describe their experiences. "It's been difficult realizing you have witnessed racism without realizing it, but once you identify it, at least you can do something next time." The underlying reality is that when white students come to understand that racism is real and is exerting a profound effect on people they care about, they want to do something about it.

For white students to get engaged in the struggle for racial justice, educators must help them learn to attune to and express their feelings. Learning about race, racism, and racial identity experience often wakes up feelings that have been systematically denied. Many white students don't have language that describes these feelings. They need to have conversations about race to help them develop language to talk about emotions.

Defensive reactions to conversations about race may include the denial of privilege or even assertions of reverse racism. Both are characteristic of a naïve stage of racial identity development and are part of the learning process. "I've never felt like I have privilege," says Ben. "My parents have worked hard for everything they have." Given time, multiple opportunities for engagement, and academic resources, Ben came to understand that privilege is a systemic phenomenon and not a personal failing. "I can't help it if I'm white," he said a few weeks later. "But I can use my privilege to help make things more equal for more people." Some students, like Harvey and Ben, who are initially resistant become staunch allies and defenders of racial justice.

Challenges to one's sense of identity can feel like attacks. For many white students, the first impulse will be to defend themselves and double down. Feeling threatened, they may want to "kill the messenger" or "blame the victim." Unless facilitators meet these reactions with patience and compassion, these students can become even more entrenched in negative attitudes. DiAngelo (2018) describes white fragility as the intense emotional reactions white people sometimes display in conversations about race. The intensity of their reactions seems out of proportion to the situation at hand. However, the intensity of their feelings is very likely proportionate to the extent to which these feelings have been previously repressed, so when such feelings come up, they may erupt like a volcano. If these students are to progress through this reactionary phase, they need space and time to deal with the intensity of their feelings. We find journaling to be effective for students who need to process feelings. Journal prompts can guide them through personal inquiries and help them acquire language to express themselves.

Because many white students are more comfortable in the intellectual domain and more accustomed to debating topics rather than dialoging, they may attempt to shift the discussion from their feelings to the mental realm. They may attempt to intellectualize, analyze, or rationalize, preferring to share opinions, beliefs, or attitudes instead of felt experience. If they come from a "head space," they may be inclined to contradict or minimize another student's experience. When Sam shared that airport security had searched his Black father's luggage while letting his dad's white friend pass through, Scott, a white student, responded, "Well, they probably catch a lot of Black people with drugs." A gentle reminder for Scott to attune to his feelings and reflect on what may have motivated his response caused him to realize that he did not want to empathize with Sam. "I don't even want to imagine how much that sucks," he said.

When white participants in these conversations begin to process the guilt, shame, anger, and sadness that frequently emerges with white identity awareness, they move into the next phase, which is one in which they feel empathy for people of color, but they may not yet understand how they can play a role in counteracting racism. This stage may include the largest category of white people and is possibly the most promising population for racial equity education. People in this stage acknowledge that people of color face racism, but they don't yet see racism as a problem for white people. They see it as a people of color problem and leave it up to people of color to "fix" it.

In another stage of white racial identity exploration, some students (and adults) do want to "fix" racism. They feel a deep desire to help people of color, but unfortunately, it often stems from a sense of wanting to restore their own sense of goodness and does not recognize the equal agency of people of color. Sometimes called *white saviorism*, this stage is characterized by a desire to help people of color assimilate into white culture rather than accepting other cultures as equal contributors to the common good. People in the white savior stage still see themselves as having superior knowledge and overestimate their understanding of racism as a systemic problem.

Depersonalizing white racial identity is a process that takes time. Initially, some students may see themselves as the oppressor and feel tremendous guilt and even shame. Recognizing that one is a member of the group that has perpetrated racism for hundreds of years may challenge their self-concepts as good people. Grappling with a social problem that is "too big to fix" may initially produce confusion and anxiety. These feelings are transitory and can be processed with time and multiple learning opportunities. The good news is that a sense of white anti-racist identity grounded in integrity awaits them on the other side of the process.

Guilt is not always a bad thing. When we feel guilt, it indicates a desire to restore love and integrity. If feelings of guilt can be channeled and processed through productive outlets – self-reflection, discussion, writing, reading, and education – those feelings can result in heightened awareness and personal growth.

White students frequently want to do something to change things, but may hesitate because they aren't sure how to "do it right." They are waiting for someone to give them a roadmap or tell them what to do. They may feel helpless and anxious during this stage of development. For high-achieving white students, in particular, who are accustomed to being the "smart one" in school, not having the answers can be stressful. In a study of race, they are often disturbed to realize how much they do not know. Because it's been necessary for their Black and Brown peers to be aware of their race, they may be at a much higher level of identity development and are consequently, more often the experts when it comes to race.

When white students come to realize the prevalence of racism in the lives of their classmates and in society, they often feel intense anger. They are angry that they have been oblivious. They're angry that it's happening. They're angry with the structures of power. We recognize that their outrage is motivated by a sense of righteousness and is a measure of their love. This is where we see students who want to dis-identify with the white race. They may blame other white people. Angela said, "I'm not like those other white people. I'm one of the good ones." They may look to people of color to assure them. Phoebe, a Black student, shared that some of her white friends see her as "the moral end all and be all about race. They want confirmation from me that they're good people."

The outrage stage is sometimes characterized as "toxic wokeness" because so often white people in this stage come across as self-righteous and judgmental. With time and continued processing, however, their anger mellows and their approach becomes less emotional and more strategic. They begin to cultivate relationships with other white antiracist allies with whom they can share their experiences. Having a network of other white allies relieves some of the burden from people of color to support and educate them.

Through continuing opportunities to explore their identities, white students advance to a stage in which they understand their white identity more deeply. They reach a point where they have a positive connection to their white racial identity and identify as both white and race conscious advocates. In this stage, they develop a desire for deeper connections with people involved in the movement for equity, both people of color and white people.

Many white students, however, arrive in our classrooms well on their way to racial identity reintegration and commitment. They are already aware, compassionate, caring, and educated. Shana started a club for white students to discuss how they could counteract racism. Royce performed a slam poem about white privilege when he was 13. At 19, he ran for school board on a racial justice platform. Don't overlook these students. They will lean into these conversations and lead the way. They can be your best allies in moving the group forward.

White identity work involves risk. For many white people, taking a stand against racism has cost them relationships with friends and families. Yet racism cripples the emotional lives of white people, and until it is unearthed and undone, it will inhibit our collective capacity to envision, enact, and embody an equitable future. Exploring white identity helps students distinguish their personal racial identities from the larger system of white racism. It offers them a path to integrity and a beloved community to live in. It helps them reclaim their full humanity. They begin to feel new energy and new possibilities. They simply feel more alive.

A Call to Educators

Undeniably, the greatest threat to building healthy relationships with students of color is the assumptions some white educators hold about them. These assumptions get in the way of them truly seeing the identities and understanding the lives of Black and Brown students. These assumptions are more prevalent than we would like to think and until they are unearthed and addressed, they will continue to prevent these educators from building relationships that guarantee the positive experiences all students deserve.

Unless white educators have done their own self-exploration work to depersonalize their white identity from the ways it's been constructed by systemic racism, they run the risk of re-centering whiteness and alienating students of color. We call on white educators to explore their own racial conditioning, develop awareness of the prevalence of unconscious bias, and learn the historical roots of racism. White educators need to understand the harm racism causes people of color, but they also need to understand how it limits the thinking of white people and robs them of human connections. Through a process of identity exploration, white educators can redefine their racial identities as those of allies, accomplices, advocates, and co-liberators. Many white educators care deeply about racial equity, and students of all races need to see this care in action.

White teachers also need to cultivate awareness to see past the socially constructed deficit narrative about students of color. They must be able to recognize the strengths students of color bring to their learning communities, affirm their intelligence, and validate the contributions of their cultures. Students of color appreciate white teachers who take the initiative to connect with them and let them know they care. They feel honored and valued by those who listen and empathize. When students of color "feel felt," it does not matter what color the person is who feels with them.

Yet students of color also need teachers who look like them, who share their experiences, and reflect their identities. Our schools need more teachers of color. Teachers of color are uniquely qualified to support students of color and to challenge white students to grapple with dissonant concepts through the trusting relationships they form with them.

All teachers need to commit to ongoing education and self-examination in matters of race. Racism is a persistent evil that harms us all, and with a clear commitment to healing racial divides, teachers see better outcomes for students of all races.

References

DiAngelo, R. (2018). *White fragility: Why it's so hard for white people to talk about racism.* Boston, MA: Beacon Press.

Friere, P. (1970). *Pedagogy of the oppressed.* New York: The Seabury Press.

Stewart, D. (2014). *Former minority students perceptions of self esteem from Atlanta K-12 Private School Experience.* Dissertation. Retrieved from http://www.inschoolspirit.com/uploads/5/1/7/8/51785713/danielle_a_stewart_final_dissertation[1].pdf

5

Creating an Identity Safe and Brave Learning Community

Mr Sanders, a Black teacher in a racially diverse public high school, organized a "culture club" for students who wanted to talk about the impact of race and racism in their lives and in their school. Only a few students showed up for the first meeting, a handful of Black students and a few white students. "I wasn't sure where to start, what to say to the kids," he said. "I wasn't sure they would be willing to say what was really going on with them. I started by asking them what they needed from each other to feel safe talking about race during our meetings. They said they needed not to be judged; they needed to trust that what they said would be believed; they wanted people to be honest, kind, and treat them as equals. They needed to know that what they said would be held in confidence and not be used as fodder for gossip. They also said they needed more people of their own race in the room to feel safe having these conversations. They needed to not be the only one."

Kiara talked about being the only Black student in her advanced placement history class.

> *I was in a group with three white guys and they were talking about how if the police pull a gun on a Black man, that he*

DOI: 10.4324/9781003191353-6

must have been doing something wrong, and that made me really uncomfortable. I didn't agree with them, but I didn't say anything. It's hard to be the only one.

Margorie, a white student said, "I'm afraid to say anything because I don't want to be seen as racist. But I do want to do something about racism."

Mr Sanders said, "I realized that if I wanted them to have real conversations, I'd have to get a diverse group of kids sitting at the table."

Our approach to community building combines social emotional learning methods with what we know from the research about the power of identity formation in learning. We use empathy-based methods to engage students in dynamic conversations with each other about their racial identities and racialized experiences. These conversations provide motivation to both learn and act.

Dena Simmons (2019, 2021) advocates for social emotional learning to be taught in the context of social justice. While many educators feel unprepared to address topics like "racism, sexism, homophobia, transphobia, and other forms of injustice that many students, particularly our most marginalized, experience daily," Simmons calls for courageous educators to embrace "Fearless SEL" and offer students opportunities to reflect on the impact of their identities. She believes Social Emotional Learning removed from the larger sociopolitical context of inequity threatens to become "white supremacy with a hug."

Transformational Inquiry is the process we use to guide identity exploration, and facilitated conversations are a part of that process. The Transformational Inquiry method scaffolds the exploration process through four domains of learning: personal, social, cognitive, and action. The goal of Transformational Inquiry is not to shape an individual's identity, but rather to facilitate a process that strengthens and broadens it. Helping students build strong identities helps them learn.

Inquiry into the personal realm is guided by questions like "Who am I?" "How do I feel?" "What am I afraid of?" "What do I hope for?" "What challenges have I faced?" "What do I believe?" "What have I learned so far?" Students explore these questions through contemplation, reflective writing, self-surveys, and other activities designed to stimulate self-study. In the personal domain, educators teach emotional awareness as an integral part of learning.

In the social domain, students share their reflections in community. They learn healthy communication skills: attentive and respectful listening, authentic self-disclosure, and how to offer supportive feedback. Teachers help them frame their identities in a positive light. They recognize their students' courage, emphasize their strengths, and reflect back to them their highest potential. Students learn from teachers how to do the same for each other. When they exchange stories and experience empathetic feedback, the deeper connections they make counteract social insecurities. In an identity-safe and brave classroom, they become more open to expressing their individuality and more capable of self-defining. "Maybe it's the trust in the classroom," says Katrina, "But I am able to express myself much more freely. I feel much safer to be myself."

The social domain is the realm of conversational learning, and students are clear that these conversations are profound for them. "Hearing my classmates stories and listening to their ideas meant a lot and made it possible for me to learn things I never would have learned before. I am so grateful to my classmates," said Laura.

These kinds of conversations inspire higher order thinking and motivate learning in the cognitive domain. In this domain, teachers help students extrapolate insights about relational dynamics to understand power, politics, and justice in the wider world. They provide materials in which students can see themselves: multicultural texts; exposure to diverse histories and cultures; and multiple perspectives. They teach reading, writing, science, math, and research skills in such a context. They guide media analysis and connect current events to their historical roots. They help students identify patterns and see social constructs that had previously been invisible to them.

Young people tell us, "It is not enough to just talk about injustice, we have to do something." In terms of identity formation, action externalizes identity through self-assertion, leadership, and community membership. Taking action completes the learning cycle, integrating the four domains of learning in the service of individual and social transformation. Action is the antidote to helplessness, isolation, and despair. Action empowers students by demonstrating that they can, in fact, make a difference.

In the action realm, educators redefine power as making a difference in the world. They encourage initiative and leadership, reward ethical behavior, and provide creative outlets for students to practice what they are learning through art, movement, drama, and other forms of play. We define action broadly, recognizing every day acts of kindness as dynamic and transformative acts. Action can mean standing up to injustice or supporting a friend. Action can take form in projects ranging from the artistic to the political: poetry slams, plays, musical performances, gallery walks, political organizing, or joining a movement. Action can mean teaching others what you have learned.

Building Relationships: Listen to Them and Teach Them to Listen to Each Other

Teachers are typically self-aware, socially attuned, and caring. They cultivate empathy and have a keen ear for listening. They honor students' thoughts and feelings, offer supportive feedback, and ask good questions. They read the room constantly to gauge interest and enthusiasm. They notice body language, facial expressions, or a shift in the quality of a student's response in class. They are genuinely curious about their students and want to learn about them. Students want to learn when they know their teacher cares.

We know that social emotional competencies support academic performance, and an inclusive classroom climate supports both. Teachers can take learning to the next level by explicitly teaching the communication skills they practice with students every day. By teaching listening and speaking skills (and providing opportunities for students to practice them), they help students make authentic connections with each other. These supportive connections foster environments in which a rich exchange of ideas can take place. In these exchanges, the power of a diverse learning community comes to life.

How can we make it safe for students to share themselves authentically in our classrooms? It helps to engage them in a norm-setting process. Ask them to generate guidelines for listening and sharing. Respectful communication skills are the building blocks of supportive relationships, and supportive relationships are the building blocks of equity and inclusion. We begin by emphasizing the importance of effective communication skills. We teach them the difference between dialogue and debate, how to listen with compassion; how to respond with supportive feedback; and how to allow themselves to be vulnerable so they can build trust in their relationships. These fundamental skills may not relate directly to racial identity, but they are key ingredients to making conversations about race effective and productive.

Research shows that at least a third of bullying is bias-related (Richardson et al., 2012). Students are frequently targeted because of their race, gender, religion, perceived sexual orientation, or physical or mental disability. Bullying is associated with high-risk behaviors, poor grades, and emotional distress, and when a core component of identity is its target, the effects are even worse.

Social jockeying is driven by social insecurity. Some students are desperate to belong, and if they can't find a healthy way to belong, they'll try to fit in through bullying, trying to be "cool," or complying with peer pressure. They're afraid they'll be ridiculed if they express their individuality, so they overconform and embrace stereotypes. This kind of posturing produces emotional alienation and results in superficial cognitive processing, a sense of apathy, and lack of interest in school. Unfortunately, these social dynamics are embedded in many school cultures.

What students need is a strong personal identity grounded in integrity. When the environment is safe for self-expression, students have more attention to focus on learning. Positive academic outcomes, especially among students of color, have been related to positive racial experiences in school (Evans et al, 2010; Howard, 2019; Leah et al, 2019). Experiences that validate a student's sense of identity emerge from carefully designed interactions between students. And teachers can facilitate these interactions.

Bringing Their Lives into the Classroom

Engaging students' real-life experiences in conversations about race makes systemic racism visible. Students can share experiences in which they have been the target of racism, witnessed it, or been afraid to stand up to it. They can share aspects of their racial identity they honor and value, like their natural hair, family histories, or activism. They can discuss how these different experiences impacted them and how they reacted when validated or invalidated. They can develop scenarios to express how they wish they had been seen and felt.

The fundamental human response to hearing a story is empathy. When students share their stories, they relate to each other and respond with compassion and respect. These conversations give them tools to identify mistreatment, find support, and learn strategies to counteract the impact of racism. Story telling cultivates empathy, fosters perspective-taking, and builds the foundation for critical thinking. When students share their stories and experience empathy in response, their "speech acts" are empowering.

Making Their Identities Visible

When we recognize the connection between the design of an inclusive culture and learning, we can use our classroom walls to reflect the identities of our students and use them as "museums" to engage them in important conversations about learning. Spence, a white science teacher in an urban middle school, was concerned about the STEM achievement gap he saw playing out in his classroom. Low performing students of color told him science was boring and checked out during his lessons. When he looked around his classroom, he saw only posters of famous white men.

Most people think of science as the domain of white men, but I knew students needed to 'see themselves' in the curriculum. And it wasn't hard to find ways to represent more diversity because all kinds of people do science.

Spence hung posters of scientists of color and women scientists on the walls. He updated his class library and challenged students to research scientists of color and women. He used his classroom walls to launch inquiries into the role of race and gender in science learning, to explore the implications of identity in the achievement gap, and to question implicit and internalized bias in the way science is performed. Students created avatars of themselves to display on an "inclusion wall," so they were surrounded by images that "looked like them" and reflected their personal and social identities as they related to "doing" science. Spence's strategies for inclusion transformed his relationships with his students. His students began to see him as a trusted advocate and sought him out at lunch and after school for those important conversations that take place outside of class.

Spence knows his students are engaged in a dynamic process of identity formation, constructing their identities in a reflexive relationship with him and with their environment. The images they see mirrored back to them influence who they may become. They need to see images that support their finest human aspirations in their classrooms, in the curriculum, and in their relationships with teachers and peers.

We can use the walls of our classrooms to affirm our students' intelligence and help them counteract stereotype threat. By creating an atmosphere of belonging, we can help them see themselves as valued participants in knowledge building. While students of color must learn to combat stereotype threat, all students need to learn to deconstruct stereotypes and critique what they see in the world around them. Respectful discussions about categories of identity can improve classroom climates and school cultures. The walls of our classroom can demarcate inclusive spaces.

Asking "What Do You Need to Feel Safe?"

We've talked to thousands of people about race. With every group we work with, we start by creating an identity-safe and brave learning community. We invite students to imagine what it would be like to feel free to say what they honestly think and feel without fear of judgment. We ask, "What do you need from the people in this room to feel safe to share your deeper thoughts, feelings, and experiences about race?" We give them time to think, sometimes allowing for long pauses.

Every group we've ever worked with – from fifth graders to eighth graders to high school seniors to educators to business executives – gives similar answers to this question. The list they generate includes acceptance, respect, honesty, courage, confidentiality, and trust. These are qualities of the heart, and they are what every human being needs to engage in authentic, meaningful, and productive conversations about race. We ask people if they can commit to upholding these qualities for each other in our conversations. Everyone always agrees. These values foster a community where empathy is more powerful than rules, and commitment to discovering truth is greater than compliance to silence.

We recommend creating a written document that outlines the guidelines for safe and brave conversations. There are multiple sources for such guidelines, and students can collaborate to develop a shared document that everyone agrees on and commits to upholding. This process helps them take ownership of their learning community. The more they participate in generating the guidelines, the more they commit to following them.

Differentiating Dialogue from Debate

We learn to debate in school, but we rarely learn how to dialogue. The communication skills necessary for equitable conversations include recognizing the difference between dialogue and debate and having the awareness to know and use the corresponding approach to achieve our intended goals. The chart below compares dialogue and debate. Where do you most often find yourself when talking about race and racism?

Dialogue	Debate
Causes introspection of one's own position.	Causes critique of the other position.
Opens the possibility of reaching a better solution than any of the original solutions.	Defends one's own position as the best solution and excludes other solutions.
Creates an open-minded attitude, an openness to being wrong and an openness to change.	Creates a closed-minded attitude, a determination to be right.
One submits one's best thinking, knowing that other people's reflections will help improve it rather than destroy it.	One submits one's best thinking and defends it against challenge to show that it is right.
Is collaborative. Two or more sides work together to arrive at a common understanding.	Is oppositional. Two sides oppose each other and attempt to prove each other wrong.
Finding common ground is the goal.	Winning is the goal.
One listens to the other sides(s) in order to understand, to find meaning, and find agreement.	One listens to the other side in order to find flaws and to counter its arguments.
Enlarges and possibly changes a participant's point of view.	Affirms a participant's own point of view.
Reveals assumptions for re-evaluation.	Defends assumptions as truth.
Calls for temporarily suspending one's beliefs.	Calls for investing whole-heartedly in one's beliefs.
Searches for basic agreements.	Searches for glaring differences.
Searches for strengths in the other position.	Searches for flaws and weaknesses in the other's position.
Involves a real concern for the other person and seeks to not alienate or offend.	Involves a countering of the other position without focusing on feelings or relationships and often belittles or deprecates the other person.

Assumes that many people have pieces of the answer and that together they can put them into a workable solution.	Assumes that there is a right answer and that someone has it.
Remains open-ended.	Implies a conclusion.

* Adapted from a paper prepared by Shelley Berman, which was based on discussions of the Dialogue Group of the Boston Chapter of Educators for Social Responsibility (ESR).

Teaching and Modeling Compassionate Listening

Facilitating conversations about race requires that you teach and model compassionate listening, explicitly outlining what listening entails: how to demonstrate respect by giving 100% of your attention; avoiding side conversations, "exchanging looks," or laughing. We teach students to pay attention to body language; to honor silences, to ask authentic questions guided by genuine concern and curiosity. We encourage them to take healthy risks: to "lean into the discomfort;" share their truths; and let themselves be known by others.

We introduce the *7 Principles of Compassionate Listening* at the outset of our sessions to reinforce listening skills. These seven principles help establish identity safe and identity brave spaces where students can dare to be vulnerable and share their authentic stories with each other.

Be fully present. When someone is speaking, give them your undivided attention. Be present and free of distractions of any kind. Listen silently. Your attention creates safety and focus for the entire group.

Listening is enough. There is no need to fix anyone or give advice. Our job is to just listen. If our minds are busy coming up with solutions, we can't truly listen with full presence. If we listen, the person sharing has the opportunity to reflect and process their thoughts and feelings, and by doing so, can generate their own solutions. Our job, as Thict Nhat Hahn says, is to allow others "to empty their hearts."

Respond with acceptance. Genuine interest and heartfelt concern make sharing one's self safe. People can be vulnerable when they sense that what they say will be received without judgment. When we ask people what they need to feel safe, the first thing we usually hear is that they need to know they won't be judged. It isn't necessary for us to agree with everything we hear. It is only necessary to suspend judgement and be fully present.

Ask authentic questions. These conversations are guided by a genuine concern to learn about the other person's life. Ask open-ended questions. "What was that like for you?" "How did that feel?" "Can you tell me more about that?" If you aren't sure that you understand what the person is trying to convey, ask for clarification. "What did you mean by that?" "Let me make sure I heard that right. Is this what you were saying?"

Recognize that conflict is a part of learning. Honest expression involves risk. We may not always understand each other initially, but if we are willing to stay connected and stick with the process, we will get there. When conflict is resolved, relationships grow stronger.

Be gentle with yourself and others. We invite you to pay attention to your own feelings, to accept whatever you may be feeling without self-judgment. Recognize that inner conflict is a natural part of learning, so if you hear something you don't like, just sit with it. Allow yourself to be uncomfortable. Allow yourself time to work through and process any thoughts and feelings that may arise. No one is personally to blame for the situation we find ourselves in about race. We have all been conditioned by systemic racism. There will be mistakes, so allow for them. Learn from them and let them go. Be forgiving. We're all learning together.

Treat the candidness of others as a gift. Students feel tremendously honored by the trust others place in them. They are capable of keeping what they hear confidential. Teach them to respond with supportive and respectful comments: "I appreciate that you shared that," or "I feel as if I understand you better now," or "I respect you for the way you handled that."

Teaching and Modeling Trust and Vulnerability

We use these guidelines to help educators and students learn how to lean into these conversations with trust and vulnerability.

Speak your truth. Be honest and open. When you reveal your story, you are giving others the gift of knowing you. Speak from the "I" perspective. Talk about yourself, and share your own feelings and experiences, and not those of others. Telling stories and relating your experiences is usually more effective than talking about abstract generalities. Stick with your feelings and avoid sharing your opinions, beliefs, or philosophies. When you tell your story, you may be surprised at how many people feel the same way you do. Even if they don't, they may respect you for sharing your authentic perspective.

Lean into the discomfort. We introduce a learning model with three psychological zones: the comfort zone, the learning zone, and the panic zone. If students stay in their comfort zones, they don't take risks, and they won't learn nearly as much. We encourage them to "lean in the discomfort" these conversations can bring up and "find their learning edge." Staying in the learning zone optimizes their potential for learning. At the same time, students need to know how to self-regulate their emotions. They need to find the boundary between leaning into the discomfort and being vulnerable and oversharing personal material and can leave them feeling too exposed. We remind them that they are never required to share their experiences. They get to set their own boundaries. They decide what they want to disclose. We advise them not to go "over the edge." We coach them on how to stay out of the panic zone, where anxiety and fear interfere with learning.

Cognitive dissonance refers to the feeling of confusion that occurs when you encounter information that conflicts with previous beliefs or "what you thought you knew." In conversations about race, cognitive dissonance is to be expected (and welcomed). Preparing students to expect cognitive dissonance help them learn to manage it when it arises. More than one student has said, "Wait! I think I'm experiencing cognitive dissonance!"

Dare to be vulnerable. Sharing one's deeper truth can feel risky. We encourage students to share themselves with each other so they can be truly known. Vulnerability and trust are intimately related. Young people want nothing more than to be heard and understood. A few brave students will lead the way, and others will follow. Almost all students find the greater intimacy that results tremendously rewarding.

Manage conflict. In an identity-safe and identity-brave environment, conflict rarely arises if students are schooled in communication skills that prepare them for sensitive terrain. But occasionally, conflict does arise, and when it does, it's crucial to redirect students to their feelings. Conflict most often arises because the conversation has become a debate rather than a dialogue, and debate is often a defense against uncomfortable feelings. When people debate emotional topics, they risk becoming more entrenched in polarized positions.

Expect non-closure. Issues of race and racism have a long and persistent history, and they will not be resolved in a single session. That doesn't absolve us from the responsibility of trying to solve them, but it would be naïve to think it will happen overnight. Racial equity requires a long-term commitment, and processing feelings associated with race takes time. It's important for students to understand that they are engaged in a process of discovery that they must go through if they are to arrive at thoughtful action. These are urgent problems, to be sure, but action bias is a symptom of privilege. Sometimes white people want to rush to fix racism. Our students need to understand that before they can solve these problems, they need to go through a process of deep learning in order to understand them. Encourage them to stay engaged, continue to question, continue to listen to the voices of people most impacted by racism, and remain open to possible solutions.

Pay attention to patterns of participation. In equitable conversations, this is a key facilitation skill. In typical classroom discourse, white males speak more than any other demographic

(Howard et al, 2006; Lee & McCabe, 2020; Pitt & Packard, 2012). Equitable conversations shift that dynamic by giving more air-time to voices from demographic groups that typically speak less. In conversations about race, students of color are our experts because they live the experience. These are the voices that need to be heard. Invite them into the conversation, make sure every-one is listening, and ensure that their experiences are affirmed and validated.

Of course, you also need to manage the students who tend to dominate the discourse. We advise students to listen ten times more than they speak. This guideline at least makes them cogni-zant of discourse power-sharing, and they will begin to regulate themselves (with a little help from their friends). There will also be the more introverted students who hesitate to participate verbally. You can invite these students into the discussion or you can ask them to respond in writing. In conversations about race, it's important to keep your finger on the pulse of what students are feeling and how they're processing the material.

Go to the source. If a student has an unresolved issue after a class session, encourage them to go to the person who is the source of their conflict to talk about it if they feel safe in doing so. If they can talk it out with each other, conflict can be resolved quickly. If they aren't ready or able to do that, ask them to come to you. They may need support in negotiating sensitive issues that arise. Sometimes conversations about race can be facilitated in small groups of students during lunch or breaks.

Practicing Generative Listening

There are three characteristics of wise teachers. (1) They see where a student is; (2) they see where a student is capable of going; and (3) they have the patience to allow the student to move from where they are to where they are going in their own way and in their own time. Generative listening involves listening to a student with full awareness of where they are, but at the same time holding a vision of the potential they have. It means

listening while seeing their emerging self with the goal of helping them connect with their highest possibilities. It's having the
patience to allow them the agency over their own growth and
learning and giving them the grace to learn at their own pace.

In conversations about race, this means seeing students as
smart and as capable of moving through their own learning
process to develop racial identities solidly grounded in integrity.
We see the potential for them to have a strong sense of self, a
strong sense of others, and a strong learning identity. We see
a vision of them they may not yet see for themselves, and we
hold the vision for them until they can hold it for themselves.
We allow them to see themselves through our eyes. We recognize
that, as Gholdy Muhammad says, "Our youths are genius. They
are not all those things that systemic oppression has created"
(Ferlazzo, 2020). We see them as geniuses, and we teach them
to see each other that way.

Conclusion

Identity and learning are intricately related. Fortunately, educators hold enormous power to mirror students' strengths and
foster their achievements. These fundamental guidelines of communication not only lay the foundation for conversations about
race, but they are transferable to any domain of life and learning
because authentic communication skills facilitate positive and
supportive relationships, and supportive relationships are the
foundation for learning gains in any area.

References

Evans, N. J., Foreney, D. S., Guido, F. M., Patton, L. D. & Renn, K. A. (2010).
Student development in college: Theory, research, and practice (2nd
ed.). San Francisco, CA: John Wiley & Sons.
Ferlazzo, L. (2020, Jan 28). Author interview with Dr. Gholdy Muhammad:
"Cultivating Genius." *Classroom Q & A with Larry Ferlazzo*. Edweek.

org. Retrieved from https://www.edweek.org/teaching-learning/opinion-author-interview-with-dr-gholdy-muhammad-cultivating-genius/2020/01

Howard, J., Zoeller, A., & Pratt, Y. (2006, Dec). Students' race and participation in classroom discussion in introductory sociology: A preliminary investigation. *Journal of the Scholarship of Teaching and Learning*, 6(1), 14–38.

Howard, T. (2019). *Why race and culture matters in schools: Closing the achievement gap in America's classrooms*. New York: Teachers College Press.

Leah, S., Matthews, C., & Harrison, A. (2019, Jan 4). Racial identity, racial discrimination, and classroom engagement outcomes among Black girls and boys in predominantly Black and predominantly white school districts. *American Educational Research Journal*, 56(4), 1318–1352.

Lee, J. & McCabe, J. (2020). Who speaks and who listens: Revisiting the chilly climate in college classrooms. *Gender & Society*, 35(1), 32–60.

Pitt, R. & Packard, J. (2012, Spring). Activating Diversity: The impact of student race on contributions to course discussions. *The Sociology Quarterly*, 53(2), 295–320.

Richardson, S. T., Sinclair, K. O., Poteat, V. P., & Koenig, B. W. (2012). Adolescent health and harassment based on discriminatory bias. *American Journal of Public Health*, 102(3), 493–495.

Simmons, D. (2019, Apr 1). Why we can't afford whitewashed social-emotional learning. *ASCD*. Retrieved from https://www.ascd.org/el/articles/why-we-cant-afford-whitewashed-social-emotional-learning

Simmons, D. (2021, Mar 10). Why SEL alone isn't enough. *ASCD*. Retrieved from https://www.ascd.org/el/articles/why-sel-alone-isnt-enough

6

Managing Emotional Processes

Janene, a white journalism teacher in a racially diverse public high school, taught her class virtually during the pandemic. Her students were disengaged, and like other teachers in her school, lack of attendance was a problem in her class. After attending our workshop on empowering student voices, Janene decided to shift gears and center the experiences of her students in her curriculum. She designed a curriculum based on the "texts of their lives" and included opportunities for them to share their experiences, particularly around their race, gender, and social class identities. In writing assignments, she asked them to share their thoughts, feelings, ideas, and experiences. She had them interview family and community members. They met in small groups to share their stories. At the end of the week, she chose a piece of student writing to share with the class.

Janene saw that her students were socializing, making connections, and learning from each other. Their engagement in school increased dramatically and so did their attendance. Remarkably, the motivation generated in Janene's class carried over to other classes, including science and math. Parents called to thank her, saying her course was therapeutic for their children at a time in their lives when they were most isolated.

DOI: 10.4324/9781003191353-7

Janene realized how often her students feel afraid of being judged, excluded, or bullied. In sharing their stories, they found out they weren't alone. They found out that other students had similar feelings, challenges, and experiences. They realized their sense of isolation wasn't because of their personal problems, but because systems of oppression kept them alienated from each other and even from themselves.

There is no magic to the art of facilitation other than a willingness to take the initiative to lead the way. This chapter delves into the heart of facilitation by exploring the in-depth process it involves. People don't change because they read a book, they change because they have an experience, and that experience has emotional dimensions. We describe how facilitators can welcome emotional expression and provide supportive feedback and cognitive reframing that moves students forward in their racial identity development.

Be Prepared Yet Flexible

Plan your road map in advance, yet be prepared not to follow it. Sometimes these conversations take on a life of their own and go in a completely different direction than you may have planned. You need to allow yourself the flexibility to follow a story that might be way more interesting and insightful than what you had on your agenda.

Recognize Your WHY

In his book, *Start with Why: How Great Leaders Inspire Everyone to Take Action*, Simon Sinek (2009) used the idea of the Golden Circle, a set of three concentric circles to emphasize the central role the question "Why" plays in transformational leadership. The question "Why" is in the center of the Golden Circle. The question "How" is in the middle circle, and the question "What" is in the outer circle. For racial equity facilitators and leaders, exploring the question "Why" leads us to clarify our values and understand our purpose for doing this work. This is where the process needs to begin. The middle ring with the question "How" focuses on the methods we will use to enact our purpose. And the third outer ring, "What" refers to the practices we will use. Most people start with the question "What," then they decide "How," and they never really get to their "Why." Sinek recommends that before deciding "What" you're going to do and "How" you're going to do it, sustainable transformation work begins with a deeper dive into the question "Why." Why is this work important? What motivates me to do it? Getting in touch with your deeper motivation is a necessary source of inspiration for racial equity work. A commitment to work within a process of racial healing is usually fueled by an educator's core values. When you are clear about your "Why," when you understand why what you're doing is important, necessary, and urgent, you'll harness the power of your passion and purpose. At that point, your enthusiasm becomes contagious. Centering your "Why" also keeps you focused and grounded when you run into obstacles, conflict, or resistance. Knowing your "Why" keeps you motivated to keep on keeping on. Danielle developed an acronym for the question WHY. "When Hope Yields," she says, "It's time to go back to your "WHY." Remember, there can be no movement without hope, and revisiting your purpose renews your hope.

The reason you do this work is likely because you saw a need; you felt a need; and you heard the needs of your students. Your personal connection to this work might take you to a deep, emotional, even painful childhood experience and that may be what ultimately inspires your work. Many teachers, especially teachers of color, are committed to making the school experience for the next generation better than it was for them. They want to offer the support they never had to the children they teach. These teachers are effective facilitators of transformation because they are connected to their "Why."

When facilitating conversations about race, it's important to remember that not everyone has the same "Why;" nor does everyone have the same level of commitment or willingness to move through the process of transformation at the same pace. One of the challenges facilitators face is getting people to commit to having these conversations. The willingness to even engage in these conversations can seem like a high stakes commitment. The emotional terrain may feel unfamiliar, uncomfortable, and unknown, and not everyone is motivated to buy into the emotional labor it takes to explore such potentially sensitive topics.

Sometimes, the first question a student asks is "Why are we here in this space having these conversations? Why is this necessary?" This question is important and the answer is telling because this is a great place to begin exploration and to start a conversation. Their uncertainties do not mean that we all cannot achieve a common goal. The goal is to gain understanding and appreciation of the experiences and emotions that bring us together. Understanding the emotions that others bring to the group will help you find the common ground for why this space is so important.

In most students, however, there is a deep longing to have meaningful conversations about issues of race, racism, and racial identity experiences. There is a deep human impulse to connect, share stories, and learn from each other. Our students want to have these conversations. Sustainable change is rooted in relationships, and these conversations provide a safe and structured way for them to discuss how they can be the best versions of themselves.

Welcome and Embrace Social Emotional Expression

Welcoming emotions into the process increases engagement. To solve the problems of racial inequities, we have to embrace our feelings and process through them. From Socrates to the Dalai Lama, great teachers have always known that transformation happens when the head and heart are integrated.

Yet we live in a society that discourages our expression of feelings, and that's especially true in education. The cultural ideology of schooling teaches us that the intellectual realm is superior to the emotional realm. We learn to avoid, if not repress, our emotions and elevate our intellects. In reality, emotions fuel the intellect, and unprocessed emotions obscure rational thinking. Repressing emotions flattens our experience of life. Bringing the emotional lives of students into the classroom, on the other hand, enlivens learning.

It's good to let students know in advance that these conversations might be emotional and that they might feel uncomfortable at times. Emotions are part of the learning process and should be welcomed and respected. Issues of fairness are intensely emotional, and talking about these issues and our personal experiences with them are bound to bring up feelings. Coming to terms with injustice can be painful, yet it is a necessary step in correcting our course.

When someone becomes emotional, our social conditioning makes us want to direct their attention away from their discomfort. Especially with young people, we often try to distract them from feelings that may be difficult. But as a facilitator, you want to gently direct their attention toward these feelings. You want them to experience and process them. You notice what they say and what they don't say. You notice body language. You notice where they pause and where their voice breaks. And you go back to what they were saying when their voice cracked, and you bear witness to that feeling.

Steinberg (2014) sees self-regulation as the most crucial skill young people can develop because it strengthens executive function and builds connection in the brain's prefrontal cortex. Providing opportunities for students to increase affective awareness helps them manage cognitive dissonance and counteract learning resistance. When we talk to students about how to find their comfort zone, learning zone, and panic zone, this language helps them regulate their emotions. Self-regulation is important for maintaining the degree of inner equilibrium that enhances learning. First, we ask them to be aware of their comfort zone. This is where they allow themselves to remain unchallenged, so if they stay in their comfort zone, they won't learn much. If they "lean into the discomfort," that's where they'll find their learning zone and optimize their potential for learning. Yet if they become too uncomfortable, they move into a state of agitation, and fall into the panic zone. We say, "lean into the discomfort, but don't lean in so far that you fall over the edge." Students begin taking responsibility for regulating their emotions, their level of emotional arousal, and their level of self-disclosure. We must respect their boundaries. We want them to be vulnerable, but we don't want them to leave class feeling that they have exposed too much of themselves. Most students are entirely capable of this kind of self-monitoring, and if they're not, teachers know when it's time to refer a student who needs additional support.

Redirect "Going Cognitive"

We sometimes see a tendency for people to "go cognitive" in conversations about race. "Going cognitive" describes the tendency to intellectualize or analyze or pontificate on one's opinions or beliefs or values instead of simply telling one's story, describing one's experience, or sharing one's feelings. Even when we advise people in advance to avoid going cognitive, they often still do it out of habit. When you're facilitating a conversation about race, and you notice a student goes cognitive, try redirecting them to their emotions. You can gently ask them to pause and reflect on what they are feeling. Or you may just notice that they "went cognitive" and make a mental note.

Move the Conversation Deeper

Genuine interest and authentic curiosity move the conversation deeper. Use open ended questions that focus attention on personal experience and particularly on felt experience. Ask questions such as: "What was that like for you?" "How did you feel?" "Can you say more about that?" or "What do you need?"

Empathy creates a state of co-resonance. We create this state of co-resonance with our presence. We see the person. We listen. We believe them. We care. We put ourselves in their shoes and see their world through their eyes. Psychiatrist Daniel Siegel (2013) describes the phenomenon of "feeling felt" or the experience of knowing someone "gets you." The experience of "feeling felt" results in healthy attachments and sets the stage for brain development. Studies on children 18 months old showed that attuned attention from caregivers resulted in development of the prefrontal cortex, the center of higher order thinking in the brain. We believe that teaching students to attune to each other also helps build their brains. Additionally, because it relies on the capacity to take another person's perspective and see the world through their eyes, resonant empathy lays the ground of higher orders of thinking, particularly critical thinking. We see the evidence in their increased capacity for higher order thinking after having these conversations and experiencing the empathy they produce. "This expanded my thinking in so many ways and made my thinking so much more open and bigger," Kristina told us.

Give Supportive Feedback

It's important to validate students' feelings and honor their experience. It doesn't matter whether you agree with their interpretation of events; it's a matter of acknowledging the reality of how they feel. This is not the time to raise questions about the veracity of events or their interpretation of events. This is a time to validate that their feelings exist and are real to them. Our job as facilitators is to acknowledge, validate, affirm, support, and encourage the felt experience of our students.

Reframe Their Stories

After a student has shared a sensitive personal story about an experience they had in the past, you can sometimes help them reframe their story by offering an appreciative perspective. This perspective should first honor their story and validate their feelings, but also call attention to their present state. Questions like "How do you think that experience has affected you?" or "What did you learn from that?" can bring them back into the present and shift the focus to what they have overcome. Recognize that no matter what our students have experienced, they have prevailed. As iChange Collaborative co-founder Oman Frame often says to his students, "Thank you for surviving that and being here with us today."

Mirror Their Strengths

We all need people in our lives who reflect back to us the highest possible image of ourselves. As a facilitator, you have the awesome power of allowing people to see themselves through your eyes. If you see the best in them, they will be able to see it in themselves. Hold a vision of their genius, their innate intelligence, and their highest potential. Sometimes as facilitators, we hold a higher vision for vulnerable students until they can see it for themselves.

Expect Cognitive Dissonance

Cognitive dissonance is a key component of learning. We advise students that they can expect to feel cognitive dissonance in these conversations, and if they stick with the process, they'll get through their discomfort and integrate new learning with what they knew (or thought they knew) previously. If students know to expect cognitive dissonance and they have a language to describe what they're experiencing, they are equipped to handle it when it happens, and we want it to happen.

Re-direct Conflict

Much of the conflict and controversy that sometimes characterize conversations about race can be averted by spending time up front establishing communication norms and community guidelines. When students participate in creating the kind of learning community they desire, they take the guidelines seriously and follow them. Learning compassionate listening skills and tools for giving supportive feedback prepare them to navigate these conversations respectfully.

If a group gets into conflict, and it does happen sometimes, you can defuse the situation by getting people to pause, take a breath, and recenter themselves. You want them to redirect their attention to the personal/emotional realm. Reassure them that these conversations are often emotional and that they are most productive when we acknowledge our feelings. These issues aren't resolved by debate and confrontation; they're resolved when people allow themselves to communicate authentically. When a student is feeling resistance, it helps to ask, "What are you feeling right now?' Bringing the focus to what the student is feeling in the present moment can move conflict toward resolution. After a moment, you can ask other students to share their felt experience in response to the conflict at hand. Getting gentle feedback from other students can help someone identify and process emotional resistance.

Manage Patterns of Silence

Sometimes it is what people don't say that needs to be addressed. Where are the silences and pauses? If people aren't talking, you need to find out why. They may not feel safe. Most of the time, silences are good. As facilitators, we tend to want to rush in and fill the silence, but we need to learn to wait. Pregnant pauses often give birth to profound insights. Give students time to gather their thoughts, formulate their words, and garner their courage so they can speak their truth. Plan activities to include introverts, such as small group activities and written reflections.

Center the Experiences of Black and Brown Students

Center the experience of your students of color in these conversations. First, listen with the intent of empowering their voices. Second, listen to learn about them and from them. They are living and breathing the politics of race every day. Racial profiling and the fear of violence is a common theme in most of their lives. In Mr Sanders' Culture Club, Brittany, a 17-year-old Black student, shared that one evening she was driving through a white neighborhood when a car with three white men began to follow her. She made several turns, yet the car continued to follow her. A Black man had recently been murdered by three white men in her town, and Brittany was terrified. Mr Sanders provided a space for Brittany to tell her story and find support from the other students, many of whom were white.

Provide a safe environment for students of color to share their experiences if they choose to and be prepared to validate their perspectives. They live close to the problem, and they are better positioned to lead the way toward solutions, so when facilitating conversations about race, follow their lead, yet protect their vulnerability.

Manage Power Dynamics

One thing to be on guard about is the tendency to allow dominant identities to control the discourse. In a conversation about race, remember that your experts are people of color. Sometimes a white person's discomfort can threaten to consume the attention of the entire group because we're used to paying attention to white people's feelings and making sure they feel comfortable. Be prepared to redirect the conversation to the experience of your Black and Brown students if this should happen.

When we survey educators in schools, we find only a small minority of educators who are entrenched in resistance. Yet often these voices are the loudest. We need to address their concerns, but please be aware that the vast majority of people we encounter are longing to have these conversations. They want to challenge racism and advocate for racial equity and justice.

Protect from Invalidation

People who share personal experience, particularly of a painful nature such as discrimination, dismissal, or aggression, need to be protected from defensive reactions. Usually when someone questions the authenticity of someone else's story, it's because they don't want to feel that person's pain or, actually, their own pain. If this happens, you can gently redirect that person to attend to their emotions. Again, it's important to keep the focus on the person who has shared their experience and not on the person who invalidates their experience. Center and affirm the feelings and experience of your Black and Brown students in these conversations.

Prepare for Patterns of Emotional Reaction

As a facilitator, it is imperative to notice the shift in group dynamics when there is an emotional charge, a common occurrence in conversations about race. These conversations can bring up different ranges of emotions in different people, and these reactions often occur simultaneously. We recognize that emotional reactions may intensify as conversations go deeper and groups step into greater levels of vulnerability. In situations like these, a facilitator might feel overwhelmed and feel as though they have lost control of the conversation. Give space to acknowledge the different emotions that are being experienced. Be mindful, however, that staying on task means continuing to move the conversation forward. Offering time for a debrief after your conversations are helpful ways to ensure that you are investing in and engaging not only what others are feeling but how they are processing what they are feeling.

We see differences in emotional reactions from those who are marginalized by their racial identities and those who are advantaged by them. This is where a facilitator must be prepared for potential emotional conflict. Black and Brown students may need the space to be heard and be able to share at a slower pace while more privileged students may be emotionally triggered to fix a problem they do not truly understand. There are distinctive patterns of emotional reactions to be aware of when you are facilitating a diverse group of participants.

Black and Brown students may have experienced racial trauma. When you are asking those who are directly affected by racism to share, there might be some resistance initially. This does not necessarily mean that they do not want to share; it means that they need to feel safe enough to do so. You will notice their engagement increase when they are given the appropriate space and guidelines which establish a safe environment. You may notice an initial reluctance to open up and share, and there may be uncomfortable silences. Then, as they begin to trust their peers, they begin to share emotions of frustration and disappointment.

In white students, we see patterns of guilt and sadness. Sometimes these feelings are masked by a sense of urgency to "fix" racism. Initially, they want to speak frequently and talk about how to find an immediate solution instead of sitting with their emotional discomfort. A facilitator can encourage these students to slow down their pace and embrace the process of compassionate listening. As these students become more comfortable with their own feelings, they speak less and listen more.

Poor intervention with either group can cause individuals not only to slow down but potentially to shut down, especially if one has felt dismissed before. Although each group you facilitate might include individuals with different perspectives and experiences, it is important to be mindful and to balance how and when participants respond to emotionally charged conversations in order to maintain the safe space necessary for effective communication and to ensure that your group is respectfully growing at a balanced pace.

Recognize Resistance as Teachable Moments

You can expect to encounter resistance and this is a good thing. This means you've created an environment that is safe enough for students to feel inner conflict and be brave enough to express it. Resistance arises from avoidance of discomfort and can take many forms. Some students want to debate the teacher or question their methods. White students may complain that the conversational method is "touchy feely" or that the teacher is blaming white people for racism. They may want to recenter white norms in schooling because they are more comfortable in the intellectual realm. Students of color may also defend white students, if they are also uncomfortable seeing their friend's discomfort.

The important thing for a facilitator to remember is not to recenter white discomfort and not allow the resistance of white students to invalidate the experiences of students of color. These white students need patience and understanding. They are grappling with new ideas. They may be attempting to deny feelings of guilt, anger, and shame. Encourage them to stick with the process. Reassure them that they are learning. and that they will benefit enormously from the process. Sometimes students who are the most resistant turn out to be the strongest advocates for racial justice. Transformational learning is a process that happens over time.

Practice Meta-Empathy

Facilitation requires split attention. While you're attending to each individual (as well as the group as a whole), while you're paying attention to body language, group dynamics, who's talking and who's not talking, you're also paying attention to yourself. Tune in to what you're experiencing in the present moment. Sometimes a simple description of what you're feeling can move a conversation along. "I am noticing my own sadness and despair right now," or "I feel so honored that you shared that story with us," or "I feel joy when I see how much you care," or "The work you're doing in this class is inspiring to me."

Be Transparent

Being aware of your own internal responses allows you to fully embody empathy. Expressing your feelings, sensations, or mental images in response to a student's story can move a conversation forward. When you express your own feelings, you model an empathetic response. Your willingness to be transparent about your own experience encourages others to do likewise. Dare to be vulnerable and model empathy and compassion.

Stay Focused on the Root Causes of Injustice

Don't be distracted by controversies over how people are protesting or how they may be denying racism. Maintain a clear focus on your "Why." Frame and reframe conversations as many times as necessary to highlight the historical roots of systemic oppression. Racism cannot be understood by well-meaning people without understanding history. A survey of U.S. history – slavery, Jim Crow, debt peonage, unfair housing practices, inequitable access to banking, healthcare, and education, restrictions on citizenship and voting rights, the rise of the prison-industrial complex – reveals the causes of systemic inequities that still plague us today. In facing our past, we can connect current social situations to the historical causes that gave rise to them. If we want students to think critically about solving persistent social problems related to racism, we have to help them examine the issue and investigate its roots.

Practice Self-care

There are many challenges to facilitating conversations about race and engaging in the work of racial equity in education. However, there are far more rewards when you feel as though you've gotten it right. Seeing your students learn, grow in compassionate understanding, and develop racial identities grounded in integrity is an uncommon gift. As facilitators, it is important to remember that as we lead and take care of others, we must also remember to take care of ourselves. As you evaluate how you perform in your role, explore how true evaluation takes place when you take deep breaths and process. Discover how to measure success through the eyes of those whom you have encouraged and in whom you have brought out the best. Your rewards come in time with the progress you see in your students. Ask yourself, "What did I accomplish?" "What worked?" "What might I improve?" "What will I carry forward in the future?"

Self-care is not easy for anyone in today's world, especially for educators. As Audre Lorde (1988/2017) says, "Caring for myself is not self-indulgence, it is self-preservation, and that is an act of political warfare." We are committed to a long-term struggle, and we have to pace ourselves. Therefore, rest is a form of resistance, especially in our culture of celebrating those who work non-stop. It is important for you to role model this behavior.

As racial equity advocates, we also go through stages of development. We begin in a naïve stage, sometimes characterized by uninformed optimism. We think the work is going to be easy and happen fast. Once we realize that's not the case, we move into a stage of informed pessimism. We're working hard and don't seem to be getting anywhere. It can seem as if for every step forward we take, we take two steps back. Sometimes we feel helpless and hopeless. If we stick with the process, however, we eventually regain our optimism, but now it is more informed and measured. We know this work is not going to be easy, but we also realize that we're going to do it anyway. We do it because it's necessary, and ultimately, it's enormously rewarding. We understand our "Why" and recognize that a commitment to a higher purpose is guiding us. We come to understand that we are not alone, that we're part of a beloved community, and we develop the capacity to find joy in the struggle.

Take care of yourself. Build your network of accomplices and allies. Your students need you.

Trust the Process

We're using the process of Transformational Inquiry, so we guide the process with questions that move our students in the direction of self-examination, personal exploration, intellectual growth, and commitment to a higher purpose. As we learn to nurture each domain of learning, we recognize that some students are stronger in the personal and social domain. They capably express their personal reflections and felt experience. Other students excel in the intellectual domain. They are analytical thinkers and problem solvers. We want to build a learning community that builds on their strengths in each area so they can learn from each other. We can provide instruction that addresses each domain so they build a balanced set of skills.

We embrace emotions because we aren't afraid of them. The authentic expression of heartfelt emotion is the most transformative thing in the world. It transforms the person speaking, and it transforms the people who are present to hear it. Authentic expression is empowering. And bearing witness to it engenders empathy, compassion, and support. We believe people are inherently capable of figuring things out. We were made to solve problems. Speaking one's truth is rewarding; telling one's story is empowering; and resonant listening is healing. As Roberto in The Color of Fear (Wah, 1994) says, "The cure for the pain is in the pain." Feeling discomfort, attending to pain, allows a light to shine in the darkness just through the power of attention. Attending to our wounds as individuals, as a community, and as a nation will allow us to heal.

References

Lorde, A. (1988/2017). *A burst of light and other essays.* Mineola, NY: Ixia Press.

Siegel, D. (2013). *Brainstorm: The power and purpose of the teenage brain.* New York: Jeremy P. Tarcher/Penquin.

Sinek, S. (2009). *Start with why: How great leaders inspire everyone to take action.* New York: Penguin.

Steinberg, L. (2014). Age of opportunity: Lessons from the new science of adolescence. New York: Houghton Mifflin Harcourt.

Wah, M. L. (1994). *The color of fear.* Berkely, CA: Stir-Fry Productions.

7

Setting the Stage for Transformation

Danielle is nervous about facilitating her first affinity group conversation with a group of teachers of color. Her greatest fear is that her professional experience in the classroom does not measure up to theirs. To prepare, she researches scholarly articles for ways to engage them in conversation. Yet during the session, a teacher stops her and asks, "Are we here to talk about how to teach or what it's like to be a teacher of color?" In that moment, she realizes that she does not have to be an expert in their field to lead them in a conversation. She does not have to know all the answers. She just needs to know the questions.

There is no one right way to prepare yourself to facilitate conversations about race and racism. You will build on your strengths, your passion, your commitment, and your own personal communication style. Sometimes, the only preparation required is to balance listening and leading with mindfulness. In addition to the logistical preparation that any facilitator should consider, it is equally important to maintain a sense of structure and to learn when and how to invite others to engage in order to maintain the flow of the conversation.

Time can be on your side as a facilitator. Therefore, learn the benefits of being patient with yourself and others. Effective

DOI: 10.4324/9781003191353-8

facilitation is accompanied by patience. Explore the growing pains, best practices, benefits, and opportunities that come with this role. Good practices for preparing yourself include getting a good night's sleep, taking time to review your notes, connecting with your co-facilitator in advance, and allowing ample time to arrive beforehand so you're not rushed. Being centered and calm is key.

It's important to prepare yourself emotionally and mentally to be present for your students before entering into conversations about race. We recommend developing a personal practice to prepare yourself. You may be called upon to hold space for pain and suffering. You may encounter feelings of sadness, grief, and anger. You need to be prepared to handle conflict should it arise. In most cases, the work you do up front to create a safe and brave environment will avert confrontation, but because this is a transformational process, you may encounter resistance to change, and being prepared to help your students negotiate this sometimes difficult terrain involves being present, knowing how to listen, and knowing how to respond in ways that facilitates deep learning and transformation. If you are not seeing resistance, you may not be helping the group delve deeply enough to create movement and learn new behaviors.

You want to prepare yourself to hold space for others. You need to be entirely, 100% present and in a place of non-judgement. You move to a place of witness, not a place of control. This state of mind is actually a place where you give up control and follow someone's story wherever it takes you. You become receptive.

Take a few moments to think about the mental field you're trying to create. We think of an inclusive environment as an energy field. Everyone has their own way of creating a safe and brave space for their students, a space as Ticht Nhat Han says, "to allow them to empty their hearts." Take a few minutes to get in the zone and reconnect with your "Why" or your purpose for doing this work.

Prepare for Who Will Be in the Room

We think about who will be in the room and the unique gifts each of them may bring. Indeed, assessing who will be in the room is a first step. Facilitating a conversation with a diverse group of students may require different activities and inquiry questions than those you might use with a same-race group. Conversations with only a few students of color in a predominantly white class-room may look very different than conversations with a group of predominantly Black and Brown students and a handful of white students. Think about how you can engage each group.

Create an Agenda

Having a clear agenda going into a conversation will help keep you on track, but we also emphasize the importance of remaining flexible. These conversations sometimes take on a life of their own and go in directions you cannot predict in advance. Balance your plan with knowledge that you may need to follow a differ-ent course. If a student tells a compelling story that needs valida-tion and process, that is more important than completing your lesson plan. If someone asks a provocative question that takes the group into a deeper conversation, be ready to shift gears.

Your agenda should include time to introduce the topic, review communication norms, and connect the students to each other. It can include facilitated activities and engage multiple domains of learning. It should include time for debriefing con-versations and activities and closing the circle.

Engage Multiple Domains of Learning

Provide activities that include several domains of learning: intro-spective or reflective questions, interactive exercises or social sharing, cognitive content that presents broad concepts, defines terms and definition, or introduces frameworks for understanding. Finally, set the stage for action by asking students how they can put what they've learned into practice.

The Transformational Inquiry Method includes four domains of learning: (1) personal/reflective, (2) social/interactive, (3) cognitive/intellectual, and (4) action/generative. Engaging multiple domains varies the stimuli keeps things interesting, addresses learning differences, and helps students integrate information. Some students are stronger in one domain than the other, so offer something for everyone.

Provide a balance of activities that involve personal reflection and introspection, interactivities exercises and opportunities for conversational exchange. The personal and social domains are the heart of Transformational Inquiry as students find these conversations and interactions enormously meaningful. We frequently hear that when they hear their own stories reflected in the stories of others, they realize they are not alone. They express relief when they understand that "they" are not the problem, and that the system of racism has made them feel isolated and misunderstood.

Make sure you provide intellectual frames for the activities you offer. An academic or theoretical frame helps connect their personal experience to social systems and gives them a context for understanding that reflects their social political world. Academic frameworks serve to legitimize and validate students' felt experiences and give direction to their passions. They integrate their emotions when they come to understand that racism is not only interpersonal, but also systemic, historic, and political. An intellectual understanding of systemic racism gives their personal experience credence when they realize they are part of a system.

Finally, because students tell us routinely that it's not enough to just talk about race, we end every conversation with a call to action. Students want to act on what they are learning, so provide opportunities to generate ideas and frameworks for action. From how to interrupt racism on an interpersonal basis to how to influence policy change to how to build movements, students will process, think, and write their way to action. They may develop action projects based on their interests, create art projects, host forums, conduct surveys, or volunteer with anti-racist organizations.

Prepare the Physical Space

Before we begin these kinds of conversations in which we bring people together to talk about their personal experiences around their racial identities, we prepare the space. We want the physical space to reflect the mindset we're trying to create. If possible, we put the chairs in a circle, so people can see each other. We pay attention to the space inside the circle and also the space outside the circle. Sonji, a kindergarten teacher, creates a centerpiece in the middle of her circle. She spreads a cloth on the floor and places flowers, a candle, or a book on the cloth. Her centerpiece provides a central focus for her students and subtly symbolizes that the space they are creating together is sacred.

If we're going to facilitate interactive exercises, we make sure people have the space to move around the room. If we're going to use small group discussions, we make sure there's space for them to break out.

Open the Circle

When you start the session, you may need to give folks the opportunity to downshift from their busy lives. You want to get them in the zone. We spend a good bit of time up front creating the space, and it pays off. Because once people feel connected and feel safe, they're way more receptive to learning.

In virtual sessions, we take time to orient everyone to using the tools available for communication, and invite everyone to be on video so we can all be seen. We might play music in the background as people arrive. When Carmen teaches virtually, she plays a piece of music a student has chosen at the beginning of class. Students often arrive early to hear whose song she has chosen and the energy is always high after the music.

Before jumping into the conversation, it always makes sense to briefly review communication norms and guidelines for a safe and brave environment.

Begin with a Mindful Moment

Take a few moments to get everyone centered. You may want to include a mindful moment in your agenda, a moment of silence, a meditative body scan, three deep breaths, or a minute of silent reflection on what each person may want to contribute or gain from the session. When you ask students to voice one word to express what they'd like to contribute to the group or what they may need from the group that day, they are participating in creating the field with the energy of their words, so this can be a powerful activity.

Create Connectedness

Start the process of getting to know your students and helping them to connect to each other. We usually include as much personal information as we can manage in the introductions. Icebreaker activities and dyads, like pair and share, not only get people up and moving, which raises the energy in the room, but they also help facilitate their engagement with each other.

We often facilitate an activity that gets students connected to each other right away. This can be a five-minute "dynamic dyad" in which students divide the time equally and practice listening and sharing with each other. Prompts like "What music are you listening to right now?" "What did it take for you to get here today?" "What do you appreciate most about yourself?" get them talking and interacting.

Sometimes inviting people to stretch or move around the room helps everyone relax and may help you get a pulse of the energy in the room.

Manage Patterns of Communication

Your role as a facilitator is to distribute communication equitably, so pay attention to patterns of communication. The goal of equitable conversations is to empower Black and Brown voices, so pay attention to patterns of discourse that typically center white voices and make sure your classroom conversations counteract these patterns. Focus on the experience and stories of your most vulnerable students. Protect their vulnerability and affirm their stories. We often create small breakout conversations where students of color are able to talk with each other. In virtual platforms, we might create specific breakout rooms for all white students to join. For in-person sessions, we use fishbowl exercises to empower the voices of students of color and give them the "critical mass" they need to tell their stories, validate each other's experience, and speak without interruption.

If someone is talking too much (and usually someone is), you need to know how to diplomatically intervene to redistribute airtime. Saying, "Thank you for those thoughts, is there anyone else want to add or share?" invites other students, who may be quieter, to speak. Make sure you open the floor to different voices. It also helps to always use a mix of both large group, small group, and personal reflection activities.

Notice Body Language

Of course, body language communicates a lot. Notice who is leaning into the conversation and who is leaning out. If a student comes in and sits outside the circle or away from the group or is looking off into space, they may feel disconnected from the group. Or they may just have something going on that day. It's

OK to stop and check in with them or at least check in during a break. People like to be noticed and called in.

Move around the Room

Circumambulation simply means moving around the circle. If there are two facilitators, we often position ourselves at different places in the circle. We sometimes sit or stand opposite each other. Sometimes our physical positions can indicate support. Moving closer can deepen intimacy. Moving away can allow space for greater autonomy in group processes.

Debrief Activities

Allow space for debriefing and to check in with how people are feeling before transitioning to the next activity. Participants process in different ways and debriefs sometimes offer "magical" moments that you can never plan for but will always appreciate. Debriefs are important. They help students integrate information and achieve closure, so be sure to allow time at the end of each activity. Debriefs can be as simple as asking students to turn to their neighbor and share a response. You can also ask the whole group to discuss one or two guiding questions about the activity. "What did you talk about in your group?" "What did you learn from that exchange?" "Did anyone have a new insight?" Sometimes we just ask, "Responses?" Students are usually eager to share their experiences and insights.

Because some students are hesitant to share their experiences openly, including brief written assignments in debriefs can help them formulate their thoughts. Ask students to write a paragraph describing feelings that came up for them and/or insights they may have gained.

It's also good to debrief the process itself. "What was it like to be listened to for five minutes without interruption?" "What was it like to look into someone's eyes?" or "What was that process like for you?" You can ask students to share insights they gained from small group discussions or from the entire conversational session. You can also ask for feedback on your facilitation or the group's process. "What worked well?" "What could have been better?" "How can we improve these conversations?"

Close the Circle

Finally, be sure to formally close the circle. You can ask students to share their main take away from the conversation, ask them to commit to an action toward change, or to share what or whom they appreciated in the session. Finally, thank them for participating and showing up with their full selves. Express your appreciation for their commitment to learning and to each other.

8

Building Your Support Network

For a long time, Danielle found it more uncomfortable to tell her own stories than to live through the trauma alone. Of course, like so many people of color, as time passed, she grew to become immune to it, she laughed about it, she tried to sometimes ignore it. Then she realized that these experiences would only paralyze her if she didn't find a space to simply "release" her struggles. She recalls, "I remember our very first virtual affinity group meeting…wigs were off, some of us were cooking, and before we knew it, strangers had become new friends." She found solace and relief from a sense of self blame that she had put on herself and the unnecessary pressure to strive to be better and to work harder just to "belong" in a society that was never designed for her to "fit" into. She began to search internally to reexamine who she was, not by society's definition, but by taking inventory of who she truly was as an individual. What she learned through the connections she made with her affinity group was that she was not alone in many of her thoughts, nor was she insignificant in any way.

Any educators involved in racial diversity, equity, and inclusion education needs a support network. Making and sustaining connections with likeminded educators is crucial to sustaining us in our work. We need people who share our passions and who we can count on to encourage our own transformational growth. We stress the imperative need for educators who are

DOI: 10.4324/9781003191353-9

leading the way in racial equity education work to intentionally build networks of connections. Although the facilitation journey is personal, you cannot do this work alone. Start by identifying the champions in your school. They might be potential accountability partners, allies, accomplices, or advocates. Establishing these relationships are not only important for you as a leader, but these are relationships of mutual exchange. The people you reach out to will recognize the value of your support and receive it as a gift.

To forge ahead in this work, you need to make meta-connections, connections based on a shared higher purpose. Find people who share your passion for racial equity and consciously and deliberately make connections with them. Make connections with people who share your identity and people who don't. We strongly advocate for affinity groups for all racial groups, but you will also need connections with people outside your identity group as well. These should be people you can count on and trust to have your back. If you don't already have a strong network of educators who share your commitment to dismantling racism, we encourage you to start building one today. Who can you talk to? Whom can you trust? Who's going to validate and support you? Who's going to take your part? Who's going to mentor you? Start making a list of your allies and potential allies. Once you have a list, take the initiative to begin cultivating relationships with them.

Leveraging the Power of Affinity Groups

Affinity groups provide spaces for racial equity advocates to connect with like-minded people. These groups provide support for people who share a common identity. They are spaces for self-care and renewal. These groups are often organic, and conversations arise naturally from participants' shared experiences. Many schools offer race affinity groups for Black, Latinx, Asian American, and race conscious white students. Some schools offer affinity groups for teachers and parents. There are also affinity groups for those who identify as LGBTQ+, women, people with disabilities, and any other group who may struggle to fit in or belong in their communities. The encouragement and support of a well-facilitated affinity group strengthens personal and collective voices. Participants also find opportunities to practice important conversations about race. They learn from each other, often sharing ideas and resources. They gain tools to build synergistic relationships, relationships that energize rather than deplete them. Some groups offer educational programs about their group's identity experience to their wider communities.

There is a certain magic that happens in racial affinity groups, and that magic can strengthen an entire organization. Even so, when building these spaces, it is important to keep in mind that you might meet with organizational resistance. Understanding the art of inquiry will help you design a group that is not only a vital resource to its members, but is also a key ingredient for solving many systemic racial challenges.

Teachers of color need same race affinities groups, and so do white antiracist educators. As facilitators, participating in and/or leading an affinity group helps us gain a better understanding of how to meet the logistical, emotional, and intellectual needs of our students and others in our communities in conversations about race.

Refueling for Educators of Color

There is a unique set of experiences for educators of color who are navigating a school system, so they face a special set of challenges. They are deeply concerned that students of color are facing the same kind of racism they faced when they were in school. They know they are qualified to lead racial equity initiatives, but also know that their abilities and qualifications are frequently underestimated and underappreciated. They may fear consequence or retribution if they speak out too strongly about racism. They could be stereotyped as "an angry Black woman" or dismissed as having a "Black agenda." When they are in leadership positions, they may feel unsupported and set up to fail.

They needed an opportunity to mourn and process the pain of racism apart from their students, parents, or administrative leadership. They need time to consider the structural changes that could improve their school. To lead transformational change, they need to be agile and responsive to unspoken dynamics.

Affinity groups for teachers of color are designed to offer spaces where participants can freely discuss the pain of racism and the toll coming to terms with its brutality takes on them. Given proper facilitation, these spaces can make a huge difference in a teacher's life who otherwise would have no network and no safe space to be validated, poured into, and encouraged. Racial equity work is exhausting and not for the faint of heart. Yet for many educators of color, the feeling of exhaustion doesn't go away. It's a way of life. "I deal with exhaustion every day," says Rachel, a sixth-grade teacher, "Not just professionally, but in my personal life too." Educators of color are standing strong, fighting the good fight against a system of racism on behalf of their students (and future generations), and not infrequently, they are encountering racism themselves. "I just want to be in a space where I can just be Black and be with other Black people who understand exactly what that means," Kim shared in her affinity group.

We strongly advocate for self-care for educators of color because we understand that, more often than not, our educators of color are the ones putting themselves out there to share their testimonies, their challenges, their pain, and their journeys with their white colleagues and students, many of whom have a strong desire to learn how to do this work effectively.

That is why affinity groups are essential to educators of color. They pour so much of themselves into this work, and no matter how exhausting the process, they continue to work hard to help others. Black and Brown educators need a safe place to debrief and refuel so they can continue to accomplish their goals and move the work of racial equity forward.

Oman calls his educators of color affinity group the "I'm not crazy club." Barbara says her affinity group "is like going to a family reunion. You might not know everyone who came, but it still feels like home." Only fellow educators of color understand the frustration in retelling countless times their painful stories about the ways race impacts them. Every person of color who has endured the pain should feel valued for the stories only they can tell.

In affinity groups for educators of color, teachers are able to let their guards down while they build one another up. This support system is essential for our work. We need to create spaces where we can strengthen our own identities, empower our own and each other's voices, mentor and support each other in resisting the impact of racism on us, so we have the energy to be present in the struggle with our students.

White Educators, Go Get Your People

One morning, Martha got a text from Oman, her iChange cofounder. The text said, "Martha, go get your people!" Oman was working in a local school that day, and, like many educators of color, he is frequently exhausted by the demands of race education work. Black and Brown educators are tasked not only with supporting students of color in a system that disadvantages them, but also supporting other educators of color in a system in which they're drastically underrepresented. Add to that the demands of white educators who call on them for academic resources, moral support, and guidance, and you have a recipe for overwhelm. These white teachers love their students and want to do what's best for them. They care deeply and have a deep desire to do something to counteract racism. They want to support their students and colleagues of color, yet they often feel confused about their role. They understand the desperate need for race education, yet they feel woefully underprepared to manage these tender conversations. A diversity director in one school told us, "I'm grateful to white educators who want to do anti-racism work, and I offer professional development and conferences, but I can't hold their hands every step of the way. What are they so afraid of?"

Indeed, white anti-racists do have a special set of issues. Talking about race is always emotional and personal, but it's also institutional and systemic. Racism is not a people of color problem. If it were, it's a problem that would have been solved centuries ago. Racism is a "white people problem," and white people need to come together to solve it.

Racial dynamics impact everyone's daily experiences, personal relationships, and life chances. People of color typically begin exploring their racial identities in childhood, giving them a level of expertise in race-related issues that few white people have achieved. White identity is often rendered invisible by the same systems of power that marginalize people of color, obscuring the ways in which racism operates on every day and structural levels. White educators need forums to explore what it means to be white and how to take responsibility for educating each other.

In Martha's affinity group for white race conscious educators, teachers have a safe place to share the unique challenges they face doing racial equity work in education. They talk about issues that aren't appropriate to discuss with their colleagues of color: the influence of childhood conditioning; the impact of racism on their own lives, unconscious bias in their families, schools, and communities; how to overcome white solidarity and break through the wall of silence; and how to find support from other white people so they don't further exhaust their Black and Brown colleagues. They share stories of their challenges and their growth, reading materials, academic resources, strategies, methods, and lesson plans they've found valuable.

Certain themes emerge from these conversations: White racial equity educators sometimes feel that they get flak from both sides. They feel dismissed by many white people who don't see the urgency of their commitment. They want to support their students and colleagues of color, but they may not know how.

They want to take a leadership role in racial equity education in their schools, but they don't want to step on anyone's toes. They're afraid of controversy and fear they'll draw criticism from administration and parents. They want to facilitate conversations about race in their classroom, schools, and communities, but feel they lack the necessary expertise. Through participating in a group with other race conscious white educators, they explore the underlying conditioning that renders them silent and build the necessary competencies to move strongly into antiracism education. They work together to gain expertise and confidence in their craft.

Sometimes white race equity educators have the desire to enact change, but they feel confusion about their role. They may feel inadequate and unprepared to have conversations about race because they are not experts. "I don't know enough," says Margaret. "And I feel guilt, maybe even shame, about being white and having privileges people of color don't have." They may feel inhibited by a fear of open conflict. They're afraid to make waves. White leaders also face repercussions for breaking with white solidarity and speaking up about race. White race activists are sometimes stereotyped as "too woke." We recommend accountability partners to help white educators gain clarity and skills for navigating the potential controversies.

White facilitators can use their communication skills to encourage school leaders and other white educators to do the work they must do to centralize racial equity education at every level of their school.

Cultivating Strategic Relationships across Differences

It's so important for us build our competencies to talk about race with their students, but also to talk about it with our colleagues. Jennifer Eberhardt (2019) says that the most effective way to counteract unconscious bias is through building close, personal relationships across differences. Growth and change rarely happens as a result of one conversation, but over time, the process of listening and authentic sharing works its magic.

For most of us, it's rare that we find opportunities to talk about race in diverse groups. Our legacy of segregation continues to haunt us, with most of our social networks still consisting of predominantly same-race folks. We must face the fact that we have inherited this legacy and recognize that it continues to operate as a systemic force in all our lives. We need to be intentional about expanding our networks. We encourage you to seek out opportunities to practice having conversations about race with colleagues and other adults in your life, both in same-race and relationship-across-difference conversations.

In a conversation with a group of teachers, Danielle invited them to initiate a conversation about race with someone they had never done this with before. Mariah, a white teacher, realized that she had never talked about race with a long time Black friend. "I don't know why," she said, "I want to know more about race in her life, and I want to grow in this area." Stephen, a Black man said,

> It just occurred to me that I have never had a conversation about race with other teachers in my school. It's just not something that I normally do. I realize after tonight that this kind of facilitated conversation is exactly what I need to be doing in my own school with my colleagues.

Indeed, it is what all of us need to be doing.

Racism is built on fear, division, and oppressive strategies that keep people apart and unable to learn about each other's common humanity. The cycle of racism has been perpetuated through a 400-year-old stream of misinformation that has established a culture of mistrust. To break this cycle, we will have to build relationships to reconnect us. These divisions can only be overcome through an intentional approach to developing collaborative relationships across differences. High-trust relationships across differences take intentional effort to build and time to sustain.

When we ask people of color what they look for in an ally, one of the first things we hear is that they look for people who talk about race. Race is often the elephant in the room that no one talks about, so white allies need to be willing not only to talk about race, but also to be willing to educates their friends and families, students and colleagues, and school communities about race and racism.

An intentional focus on building relationships across difference will be necessary to transform individuals and systems. These relationships can be strengthened by defining our relationships and clarifying our boundaries. We may not be necessarily be friends and hang out on the weekends, but we are strategic partners and may operate as allies, accomplices, co-conspirators, and, yes, sometimes as friends and radical kin.

If conflict arises, that can also be managed strategically. The first rule is, if possible, go to the source. The fewer people involved the better. When conflict is resolved, it strengthens relationships, and even when it's not, it clarifies the boundaries in a relationship. And having clear boundaries strengthens your identity. You don't have to work with everybody. In doing racial equity work, you get to work with people who respect and support you, no matter what color their skin is.

Sometimes teachers tell us they don't even know each other, much less know how to support each other. Micro-inclusion practices are a good place to start. There's enormous power in a warm greeting, a smile, or a hug. Some teachers host lunchtime mixers in their classrooms, inviting people they might not ordinarily connect with to share conversations over a meal. Some schools use relationship building activities to start faculty meetings. The important thing is to be intentional. We encourage you to reach out to others, find your people, and allow yourself to be known. So many rich and wonderful relationships await you.

Reference

Eberhardt, J. (2019). *Biased: Uncovering the hidden prejudice that shapes what we see, think, and do.* New York: Viking.

9

Preparing to Launch and Lead

In our Racial Equity Institute, we ask a group of Black women what it is like for them to be educators.

"In situations with mostly white people, I second guess myself," says Alisha. "I'll ask myself, 'Did they not say hello to me or not shake my hand because I'm Black?'"

"I get that," says Christina. "I have taught myself to feel superior. I know I have to be the smartest person in the room. It's the same old 'you have to work twice as hard just to get half as far.'"

Monica shares, "I hear in my mind, 'Don't be a victim.' I know I have a lot of privilege, but when I walk outside my door, people don't even look at me."

"People expect us to be strong," says Erica. "But I don't always feel strong."

"Being a Black woman is one of the hardest things in the world," comments Denise. "But I wouldn't trade it for anything. We are the holy grail of people. I have to remember that regardless of what other people think of me, I know who I am."

"And I know why I'm here," Christina adds. "I'm not here just for myself. I represent family members, community members, and so many others who came before me and sacrificed so I could be here. I represent so much more than just myself."

DOI: 10.4324/9781003191353-10

"I'm here for the kids," says Alisha. *"I know they need me, and that's what keeps me going."*

The women in this conversation exemplify transformational racial equity leadership. These women of color, whose experience at the intersection of racism and sexism defines much of their professional experience, have necessarily explored and come to terms with their racial identities. The rigorous process of identity exploration they have necessarily engaged in has required a deep analysis of race on personal, interpersonal, intra-group, and institutional levels. Their effort has empowered them resist the impact of racism to some extent. Their sense of racial identity has grown strong, and their sense of self is grounded in ethical values. They are clear about the core integrity of their being. They have arrived at a mature stage of identity characterized by a sense of purpose and are committed to a cause greater than themselves. They are change agents, driven by the need to make the world a better place for the generations coming after them. Their thinking about race is well-developed and strategic. They are in the identity achievement zone, and they are leading the way toward transformational change.

In conversations about race, it's important to listen to the folks most impacted by the problem of racism. In our experience, listening to the lived experiences of Black women has been a game changer for so many people. Equitable conversations are not conversations in which time is equally shared, but are rather conversations that empower the voices of people of color and coach others in the art of listening.

Racial Identity Achievement and Transformational Leadership

Born out of an intense process of self-examination, racial identity achievement is a state of reintegration and commitment. It is a state of proficiency, characterized by a deeper understanding of one's self and the world one lives in. A person gains a sense of agency which gives them the power to self-define rather than be defined by others. They move beyond the ego and think independently. They see themselves as part of a larger whole and can abstract their identities from the systems surrounding them. They have acquired expert knowledge and are confident in who they are.

Like the women in the conversation above, transformational racial equity leaders have often gained their identity strength through the process of facing and overcoming racism. They have transmuted their pain into power. These are the educators who are fearless in conversations about race and are equipped to guide their schools through the change process.

Transformational racial equity leaders must be passionate about their cause because the demands of the work are relentless. They must have courage because the risks are high. They must have confidence because their values will be tested. They must have compassion because only a deep sense of care can guide them. They must collaborate with others because no one can do this work alone.

The problem is that because of the barriers of systemic racism, we have too few people at this stage of development. When more people of all races arrive at the stage of racial identity achievement, we will see racial transformation on a larger scale.

Levels of Racial Identity Development among Educators

In your work as a facilitator and a transformational racial equity leader, you will encounter individuals along a wide spectrum of development. We typically find ourselves in the room with people of color who've done extensive racial identity exploration work. Because their sense of self has been challenged by racism, they've had to work hard to maintain their sense of self-worth, and consequently, they've acquired a level of proficiency that few white people understand. In the same room, we may have people in the very early stages of racial identity development. These people may be just beginning to explore their racial identities and don't yet understand the impact their identity experience has on their student or colleagues. Sometimes people say "I don't see color" without understanding the implications of that statement. And while such an attitude may be well intentioned, it's not acceptable in an educator. Educators have a responsibility to be aware of the role racial identity plays in their students' life experience and how it impacts their learning. Educators need to be accountable. Otherwise, they risk perpetuating racial disparities no matter what their intentions may be.

Teachers in the initial stages of racial identity development need professional development programs designed to raise racial literacy. They have a lot to gain by exploring their own identities, addressing the role their social location plays in their teaching, and understanding differences in patterns of identity experience. At the same time, educators in the more advanced stages of racial identity need programs designed for people who have already done the deep analysis. These programs can provide a pipeline to school leadership because these are the people who are ready to move the process forward through initiating structural change.

Leadership Liability

Student populations in schools today are more diverse than ever, but the diversity of the teaching force lags behind nationwide. In 2017, students of color made up 52% of the K-12 public schools population. Latinx students made up 25% of the population, Black American children were 15%, Asian groups constituted 6%, and American Indians made up 1%. Yet in the same year, 79% of K-12 teachers in the United States were white and 76% were women (Characteristics of public and private elementary and secondary school teachers in the United States 2020). The majority of these teachers (65–70%) are white women (El Mekki, 2016; Penick-Parks et al, 2018; Toldson, 2011). Fewer than 7% of teachers are Black and less than 2% are Black men. For every 534 Black male students, there's a teacher who looks like them. For every 15 white female students, there's a teacher who looks like them (Lewis & Toldson, 2013).

Because of the disproportionate numbers, teachers of color bear a disproportionate burden. There is a certain level of liability leaders of color incur, not because of a lack of capability, but because of a lack of support. Similar to school leadership, educators of color are also charged to lead the change toward racial equity in schools where they may not even be invited to sit at the decision-making table. While the people most impacted by racism are in the best position to know how to solve the problems arising out of racism, they are often not in positions of power. Right now, the racial equity movement in schools is being "led from behind," with top school administrators often being the most difficult people to get onboard for this work. Janie, the diversity director at her school told us,

> I was appointed diversity, equity, and inclusion coordinator at my school after there were some racial incidents, but I now realize that my administration is not interested in making any real changes. I don't even have a budget. Clearly, I was only put in the position for the sake of appearances. How am I going to tell my students of color that the promise of change the school made to them was an illusion?

In addition to their normal course load and other teaching responsibilities, many educators of color find themselves in the position of supporting students who encounter discrimination, microaggressions, unconscious bias, and racialized insults. And keep in mind that while they're supporting students, they may also be protecting themselves from discriminatory encounters with their colleagues, students, and parents. They're also called on to negotiate misunderstandings between white teachers and students of color, as well as between students. White teachers come to them for advice on how to manage students of color, and teachers of color are expected to mentor white teachers in race related issues.

Teachers of color report feeling isolated, unsupported, and overlooked for leadership opportunities. Even though they may be recruited for equity-related reasons, they're not mentored or given a voice to do racial justice work. This adds to the already significant problem of teacher burnout. Teachers of color leave the teaching field at higher rates than white teachers (Borman & Dowling, 2008; Davis et al., 2019: Dilworth & Coleman, 2014; Nguyen, 2020). This trend is increasing with the contentious national debate about critical race theory. Frustrated and exhausted teachers of color are leaving education careers in record numbers. Unfortunately, this trend has profound implications for the overall state of education because research shows that not only are teachers of color more effective at closing the racial achievement gap, but they are also rated highly by students of all races.

Making our schools responsive to the needs of teachers of color will require a significant culture shift. The first step is to acknowledge the problem and recognize that teachers of color are carrying an extra burden and may be experiencing racial battle fatigue. They need institutional support that compensates them for the extra work they're called on to do.

We need to see more schools commit to hiring, retaining, and advancing the careers of educators of color. Students of all races benefit greatly from having teachers of color and so do their colleagues. A study (Unrealized Impact, 2017) found that teachers and staff of all races are three times more likely to recommend organizations they see as diverse, equitable, and inclusive. People of all races, but particularly people of color, are more likely to stay in organizations they perceive as diverse, equitable, and inclusive. A focus of school should be to create cultures that welcome, appreciate, and advance the careers of educators of color.

Listening Leaders

Most organizations take a top-down approach to change leadership. They create policies at the executive level and then cascade them down through the organizational hierarchy. With transformational racial equity leadership, however, the rules are a bit different. Transformational racial equity leadership is not dependent on your position in a hierarchy. It's dependent on the expert knowledge you've gained from examining your life experiences. Thus, cultivating the capacity to listen to voices and hear the stories of the people most impacted by racism is the single most important characteristic of a transformational racial equity leader. Listening leaders ask more questions and give fewer answers. They explore their own conditioning. They recognize the inevitability of conflict and build their capacity for discomfort as they learn and practice critical communication skills in conversations about race. They intentionally cultivate same-race connections and build relationships across differences. They learn to hold space for defensiveness, anger, and guilt, both within themselves and for those they interact with. They practice cultural humility by knowing that they cannot do this work alone.

Leading from Wherever You Are

Everyone can lean in and lead transformational change. You can focus on your own sphere of influence in your teaching practice, your work as a counselor, or as a school administrator. Transformational leaders lead from wherever they are because they are inspired. Their passion for justice and enthusiasm for equity are contagious and, in many cases, they exert a magnetic force that attracts people to them.

The facilitation skills we present in this book are practices you will incorporate into your day-to-day relationships everywhere – in the hallways, in the lunchroom, in your faculty meetings, and in the teachers' lounge. You will model them for your students in your classroom, and your students will take them beyond the walls of your school. They will take the knowledge and skills they learn from you and initiate transformational conversations in their own lives with their friends, their families and in their communities.

When you facilitate conversations about race, you are by definition a racial equity leader. Transformational change begins with conversation. Cultural critic bell hooks (2015) says that conversation is the revolutionary way of learning. Grace Lee Boggs (2012) unequivocally states that conversation IS activism. The foundation of equity lies in mastering the art of authentic and equitable conversations. These conversations build community in the classroom and beyond. By creating these spaces for your students, you allow them to share their joy and pain, to feel seen and heard. They will respond with courage and hope. They will work hard because they know their work matters. They will emerge as leaders themselves. So, you are not only leading the way for change yourself, but you are empowering the changemakers of today and tomorrow.

Redefining and Claiming Your Power

In the Transformational Inquiry method, questions of power are always at the core. Who produces these fields of identity and why? In what ways are certain bodies weighted with differential life chances? Who is empowered and who is disempowered by these identities? How are our identities shaped by society and how can we exercise more autonomy over our identities?

People with power have the opportunity to shape their lives and the larger world around them. According to Dr Martin Luther King, Jr, "Power properly understood is nothing but the ability to achieve a purpose. It's the strength required to bring about social, political, and economic change" (King, Jr, 2013). Learning to see and understand power relationships is vital for personal and systemic change.

To understand racial equity leadership, we must redefine power and distinguishes "power over" from "power with." "Power over" is a top down, hierarchical model of power that seeks to command and control others. "Power with," on the other hand, seeks to empower others through mutual support, respect for differences, and collaboration. Transformational power integrates the head and the heart. When a deep sense of care fuels the thought process, the outcome is a capacity for higher order thinking. The process of rigorous identity exploration depersonalizes identity constructions based on dominant culture norms and allows individuals to see the interrelated systemic nature of social disparities. Once that realization is achieved, thinking develops ethically and action becomes strategic.

Learning to see, name, and understand power relationships is vital to transformational change. We need to rethink what power means and explore how it operates in our lives, relationships, and institutions. We need to ask how we can use the power we have in purposeful ways. Alice Walker says, "The most common way people give up their power is by thinking they don't have any." Indeed, most people have more power than they think. We need to identify where our power lies and define our sphere of influence. We must begin to think of power as a dynamic, interdependent, and fluid system of relationships, instead of a fixed hierarchy. When we see, name, and claim the power we have, we are in a better position to leverage our power to achieve a greater purpose.

Transformational leaders believe that purpose of education is to transform society. Their aim is to empower students to think for themselves, to learn what they most need to know, and to develop the agency to act in their own interests and in the interests of others through acts of solidarity. Education at its best supports students in developing the knowledge, skills, and vision to transform the world.

References

Boggs, G. L. (2012). *The next American revolution: Sustainable activism for the twenty- first century.* Berkeley: University of California Press.
Borman, G. D. & Dowling, N. M. (2008). Teacher attrition and retention: A meta- analysis and narrative review of the research. *Review of Educational Research, 78*(3), 367–409.

Characteristics of public and private elementary and secondary school teachers in the United States: Results from the 2017–18 National Teacher and Principal Survey. (2020 Apr). *National Center for Education Statistics.* Retrieved from https://nces.ed.gov/pubs2020/2020142.pdf

Davis, D., Griffin, A., & Teoh, M. (2019, Sep). If you listen, we will stay: Why teachers of color leave and how to disrupt teacher turnover. *The Education Trust.* Retrieved from https://edtrust.org/resource/if-you-listen-we-will-stay/

Dilworth, M. E. & Coleman, M. J. (2014). *Time for a change: Diversity in teaching revisited.* Washington, DC: National Education Association.

El Mekki, S. (2016, Jun 8). Why are over 70% of our teachers white female? *Philly's 7th Ward.* Retrieved from https://phillys7thward.org/2016/06/why-are-over-70-of-our-teachers-white-females/

hooks, b. (2015). Moving from pain to power: Choosing the space of radical openness. Scholar-in-Residence Program, Eugene Lang College of Liberal Arts, The New School, New York. Retrieved from www.youtube.com/watch? v=cpKuLl- GC0M

King, Jr., M. L. (2013). *The essential Martin Luther King, Jr.* Boston, MA: Beacon Press.

Lewis, C., & Toldson, I. (Eds.). (2013). *Black males teachers: Diversifying the United States' teacher workforce.* Bingley: Emerald Group.

Nguyen, M. (2020, Apr 16). *Pipeline and retention of teachers of color: Systems and structures impeding growth and sustainability in the United States.* Digital Promise. Retrieved from https://files.eric.ed.gov/fulltext/ED610745.pdf

Penick-Parks, M., Moore, E., & Michael, A. (2018, Aug 31). Understanding: The first step for white women teaching Black boys. *Teaching Channel.* Retrieved from https://www.teachingchannel.com/blog/white-women-teaching-black-boys

Toldson, I. (2011). White women are 63 percent of the teaching force. Can they teach black boys? Excerpt from: Men in the classroom. *Living Education eMagazine.* Retrieved from www.youtube.com/watch?v=VYo9i1Hccpl

10

Epilogue

In a session with educators in a predominantly white school, a teacher described an incident in which a student had used the n-word during class. The administration had disciplined the student, and the disciplinary action was currently the "talk of the campus." When we asked these teachers how they were addressing the incident with their students, we discovered that only one of them, Marissa, a Black teacher, had talked with her students about it. Marissa had contacted the Black students who were present when the incident happened and offered them support. She had talked to her class about the pain the word causes and gave them some history about the word. Corrie, a white teachers said she was hesitant to bring it up with her students. She didn't know if it was her place to have these conversations with students, and she didn't feel prepared to guide them. Laura, another white teacher, said she was afraid of pushback from students and parents. She just didn't know how to respond.

When we ask teachers in our Race Equity Institute how many of their schools have dealt with incidents involving the n-word or similar racial slurs in the past year, almost every hand goes up. Teachers frequently describe scenarios in the classroom and on the playground in which students use the n-word. When we think about ways to intervene in order to minimize the trauma these incidents cause, we must understand that they can leave

DOI: 10.4324/9781003191353-11

long-lasting harm. We must take them seriously and never minimize their impact.

These incidents present us with teachable moments, and we need to be talking to students about them. It's not enough to tell them not to use the word or discipline them when they do. Students often don't understand the harm the word causes. When Danielle coached a white high school student who had used the word "to get a stupid laugh" from his classmates, she recognized that he didn't understand the weight this word carries and needed to be better informed. She shared a story from her childhood about being called the n-word on a soccer field by a boy on the opposing team. She described the pain, humiliation and guilt she felt, as if she were in some way responsible. Once he understood, he committed to never use the word again and to advocate against its use.

In Danielle's case, her mother immediately approached her white coach and asked him to intervene. If her mother hadn't reacted just as quickly as it happened, her coach might not have even responded. As humiliating as the incident was, seeing her coach stop the game and demand a public apology reassured her that she had done nothing wrong, and it let her know that she was not alone. In that moment, the adults surrounding her were accountable. While the pain she felt that day is still present, it has resulted in her commitment to helping educators understand that we cannot afford to take these incidents lightly, and we must address them with students. "Today I represent not only a professional race educator, but a child who was harmed and yet overcame that harm by having the right kind of support from the adults in my life."

Calling All Educators to Action

We all have a role to play in educating students about the power and politics surrounding race, racism, racial identities, and the resulting patterns of experience that accompany our identities. It begins with educators being prepared to talk with students, being accountable to students who have been harmed, and holding students accountable who have caused harm. We must understand how to respond to each with compassion and guidance.

It's so important for everyone in the education profession to build thier competencies to talk about race with their students.

Facing Backlash

In the midst of the 2020 pandemic, the tragic murders of George Floyd, Breonna Taylor, Ahmaud Arbery, and countless others, inspired a movement for racial reckoning. Yet in the wake of that movement, the forces of backlash manifested almost immediately. Laws designed to criminalize protesters and restrict voting rights were introduced in state legislatures across the nation. Responding to a campaign to ban the teaching of critical race theory, lawmakers in more than a quarter of states attempted to pass restrictions that govern how teachers can talk about race and racism in their classrooms.

Critical race theory, which is rarely taught outside of law schools and graduate levels in education, is a way of looking at racism that questions why, after so many centuries, racial disparities persist in the United States. CRT argues that these disparities are embedded in U. S. legal institutions (the criminal justice system, education, labor, housing, and healthcare, among others) through laws and government policies. The anti-CRT backlash narrative mischaracterizes the CRT framework and promotes fears that children will be taught that all white people are oppressors and all Black people are hopelessly oppressed victims. The tenets of CRT, however, do not suggest that white individuals living today are to blame for the racial disparities these laws have produced. CRT, a framework for systems thinking, depersonalizes individual white identity from the structures of white supremacy.

While in actuality, we know of no K-12 curriculum based on critical race theory, conservative think tanks funded by wealthy elites have drawn tactics from the oldest playbook in politics:

breed racial resentment to maintain power at a time when a multiracial democracy is rapidly emerging in the United States. Most attackers of critical race theory cannot define it, yet anti-CRT bans threaten teachers with job loss and certificate revocation if they teach concepts such as white privilege, implicit bias, intersectionality, structural racism, and even social emotional learning. Some state laws hold school districts liable if teachers make white students feel uncomfortable about their race.

We are amazed to learn that school leaders sometimes aren't aware of the work teachers in their midst are doing behind the scenes. Despite challenges and lack of support, these heroic educators continue to lead with their hearts on behalf of the children they teach. Most teachers tell us that in the midst of this national controversy, they are doing what they've always done. Elementary teachers continue to normalize differences in skin color, teaching empathy, respect, and compassion for differences. Middle and high school educators continue to teach that governments are systems and allow the historical narratives of the Civil War, Reconstruction, the rise of white supremacy during the Jim Crow era, and the Civil Rights Movement to demonstrate the systemic nature of racism. Meredith, a high school history teacher, says it's impossible to teach current events without discussing how the history of race affects the world now. English and language teachers continue to introduce their students to narratives written by authors of color and facilitate discussions about how race, racism, and racial identity impacts the characters' lives and their students' lives.

It's easy to lose sight of why you signed up to do this work when you encounter resistance, yet we encourage you to remember that resistance is not necessarily a bad thing. We have found that those who resist change have their own set of fears about the loss of power and identity. Their resistance may not be so much about challenging you as it is about them being challenged by the change process. When these individuals challenge your work, you must remember that.

As a white child raised in the segregated South, Martha was a part of the backlash against the Civil Rights Movement, so she understands from firsthand experience how the ugly and self-destructive forces of racism create a backlash effect. The narrative of white supremacy was all she had ever known until her school was forcibly integrated. Her worldview was suddenly challenged by the integrity and intelligence of the Black children she encountered. At night, she watched footage from civil rights protests around the nation flash across her television screen. Yet her initial response, like that of many white people in a naive stage of racial identity development, was to become more entrenched in her segregationist position. With repeated exposure to these undeniable images of human dignity, however, she could not resist the moral force of the truth. She came to understand that far from being harmed, white people will reap tremendous benefits – materially, emotionally, mentally, and spiritually – from the solidarity dividend they will receive when racial disparities are alleviated. She learned that there are limits to what violence and repression can accomplish, while the truth is a force more powerful.

As racial equity leaders, we understand that facing backlash requires courage, stamina, and strategy. We are engaged in a game of chess, not checkers. We can't allow ourselves to be distracted by the noise of misinformation, and we can't allow ourselves to personalize these attacks. We have to find the courage to meet resistance with compassion. We have to keep our eyes on the prize and our hearts centered in the love of truth. Coming to terms with racism is an emotional process that requires facing a history of cruelty. While it is not the fault of any one individual living today, it is a moral imperative for everyone living today to begin the process of healing the past to create a better future. The truth is a force that is destined to inspire a new generation.

Moving Forward: Key Strategies

Let's review some of the key developmental strategies for facilitators we cover in this book. This set of competencies will position you to facilitate conversations about race and then leverage the themes that emerge from the lived experiences your students to build curriculum that further enhances learning.

- ◆ *Start with the "I."* Explore your own experience and understand how you have been impacted by interpersonal, internalized, intra-group, and institutional racism. Reflect on your upbringing, begin the process of uncovering your unconscious bias, and recognize the ways you've been empowered and/or disempowered by your racial identity. Only through an ongoing process of rigorous self-exploration can you understand impact of systemic racism on every single one of us in every aspect of our lives.
- ◆ *Center your "WHY."* Get clear about your purpose. It will center and guide you. Ask yourself these questions: What led you to this place? Why do you believe these conversations are necessary? Why should you be the one to lead them?
- ◆ *Educate yourself.* Understand the impact of racial identities on teaching and learning, and know how your own identity impacts your students. Learn the history of race, especially the history of race in your subject area. As an educator and facilitator, it is essential to fully know the history of racism and direct the conversations to stay focused on the root causes of injustice. Dig in to deeply to understand racial privilege and the impact of dominant conditioning. Remember, this is a marathon, not a sprint. We are here for the long haul, and this work requires continuous education.
- ◆ *Create identity safe and identity brave learning communities.* Teach respectful communication skills that foster relationships. Teach students to listen with compassion and respond with empathy. Provide instruction on emotional and social literacy. Reward them for their emotional labor and acts of compassion, as well as for their intellectual labor.
- ◆ *Use the Transformational Inquiry Method.* Recognize that young people are deeply concerned about issues of

fairness and justice. Support them in developing the knowledge, skills, and vision to transform the world they live in. To guide them through a transformational process, engage multiple domains of learning. Offer them opportunities for personal reflection. Facilitate conversations and activities that structure respectful social interactions so they learn important dialogic skills. Provide intellectual frameworks and academic resources to strengthen their intellectual understanding of race, racism, and racial identities. Provide opportunities for them to demonstrate what they are learning through purposeful and deliberate action. Action externalizes identity through self-assertion, leadership, and community membership.

◆ *Recognize, validate, affirm, and empower racial identities.* Represent a diversity of racial identities on your walls, in your halls, and throughout your curriculum. Center authors, experts, and role models of color. Present narratives that amplify voices of color and exemplify the strengths and gifts of communities of color.

◆ *Bring students' lived experience into the classroom.* Integrate students' lives outside of school with what they are learning in school, particularly students of color. Get to know your students both inside and outside the classroom. Create platforms for them to tell their stories and be empowered by the experience.

◆ *Take an intersectional approach.* Recognize the centrality of race as an organizing principle of society, but also acknowledge that we are all individuals who are more than just our race. Be aware that racial identities intersect with other aspects of identity such as gender, sexuality, ethnicity, language, age, religion, and abilities. Different aspects of students' identities are more salient at different times and in different contexts.

◆ *Include and involve families and communities.* Bring parents and caregivers into the conversation through assignments that include them. Ask for their input and invite them into the classroom to tell their stories. Bring in guest

speakers from students' communities and find ways connect students to people who share their passions.
◆ *Prepare yourself for resistance.* The current national controversy about race in education is nothing new. Advocates for racial justice have always faced backlash, and
they expect it. They know it's part of the long game. Lead
with the truth. Systemic racism is a fact that can is dem-
onstrated by a survey of "hard" history.
◆ *Remember that you're a part of a movement.* In Sanskrit,
Satyagraha means "Truth Force." As Martin Luther King,
Jr. said, "We shall overcome because the arc of the moral
universe is long but it bends toward justice."

Conclusion

For Danielle, facilitating conversations about race was not a
role she envisioned for herself. It wasn't until others naturally
gravitated toward her and asked her to lead these conversations
that she began to ask herself why these opportunities continued
to find her. What she discovered is that a true leader is not only
a person who is willing to take on the task, but that leadership
is often a reflection of the gifts others have recognized and cultivated in you. She wanted to pass on the gifts that others had
passed to her, and she realized that if we are ever to achieve
justice, change and progress, she, along with many others, would
be required to step up and lead.

She frequently begins the conversations she facilitates with
the million-dollar question: "Why are you here?" This question reveals where people are on their racial journeys, and their
answers to the question reveal their individual and collective
purposes. Often "someone or something" has inspired them to
show up and to join in these conversations. "Why?" is one of
the most powerful questions you can ask in this work. Knowing
why we are here and staying true to our purpose will keep us on
the right track. When Hope Yields, go back to your "Why." This
will be your reminder to persevere. Your "Why" will re-center

you, refocus you, refuel you, and reignite you and your facilitation super powers.

With each conversation about race, our world comes closer to being a kinder and more equitable place. Remember, you don't need to know all the answers, because knowing how to ask the right questions is what guides the process. There is no right or wrong way to facilitate these conversations. With practice, you will develop your own methods and find your own style. Keep in mind that listening with compassion and responding with empathy are truly the most important skills you need.

Leading conversations about race might well be one of the most challenging, uncomfortable, and hardest roles you will serve in. However, for many of us, this work is a labor of love – a love of justice, a love of humanity, and a love of hope. So much hope is needed during this time of uncertainty and continued disparities. You are very likely in the right place at the right time to do this much needed work. So, after you ask yourself "Why?", ask yourself, "Why not?" (King, 1968).

Reference

King, Jr, M. L. (1968). "Remaining awake through a great revolution." Speech given at the National Cathedral, March 31, 1968. King Institute. Retrieved from https://www.learnoutloud.com/Free-Audio-Video/History/Speeches/Remaining-Awake-Through-a-Great-Revolution/90598

Printed in the United States
by Baker & Taylor Publisher Services